The
PD Curator

The PD Curator

HOW TO **DESIGN**
PEER-TO-PEER
PROFESSIONAL LEARNING
THAT **ELEVATES TEACHERS** AND **TEACHING**

Lauren Porosoff

ASCD Alexandria, Virginia USA

1703 N. Beauregard St. • Alexandria, VA 22311-1714 USA
Phone: 800-933-2723 or 703-578-9600 • Fax: 703-575-5400
Website: www.ascd.org • E-mail: member@ascd.org
Author guidelines: www.ascd.org/write

Ranjit Sidhu, *CEO & Executive Director;* Penny Reinart, *Chief Impact Officer;* Stefani Roth, *Publisher;* Genny Ostertag, *Director, Content Acquisitions;* Susan Hills, *Acquisitions Editor;* Julie Houtz, *Director, Book Editing & Production;* Jamie Greene, *Editor;* Thomas Lytle, *Creative Director;* Donald Ely, *Art Director;* Georgia Park, *Senior Graphic Designer;* Keith Demmons, *Senior Production Designer;* Kelly Marshall, *Manager, Project Management;* Shajuan Martin, *E-Publishing Specialist;* Christopher Logan, *Senior Production Specialist*

PAPERBACK ISBN: 978-1-4166-2990-0   ASCD product #121029   n3/21
PDF E-BOOK ISBN: 978-1-4166-2991-7; see Books in Print for other formats.
Quantity discounts are available: e-mail programteam@ascd.org or call 800-933-2723, ext. 5773, or 703-575-5773. For desk copies, go to www.ascd.org/deskcopy.

Library of Congress Cataloging-in-Publication Data

Names: Porosoff, Lauren, 1975- author.
Title: The PD curator : how to design peer-to-peer professional learning
   that elevates teachers and teaching / Lauren Porosoff.
Other titles: Professional development curator
Description: Alexandria, Virginia : ASCD, 2021. | Includes bibliographical
   references and index. | Summary: "The PD Curator is about how
   professional learning experiences can become more inclusive,
   participatory, cohesive, and effective-and about the role teachers and
   leaders can play in creating those experiences"-- Provided by publisher.

Identifiers: LCCN 2020051932 (print) | LCCN 2020051933 (ebook) | ISBN
   9781416629900 (paperback) | ISBN 9781416629917 (pdf)
Subjects: LCSH: Teachers--In-service training. | Teachers--Professional
   relationships. | Mentoring in education. | Career development.
Classification: LCC LB1731 .P64 2021 (print) | LCC LB1731 (ebook) | DDC
   370.71/1--dc23
LC record available at https://lccn.loc.gov/2020051932
LC ebook record available at https://lccn.loc.gov/2020051933

30 29 28 27 26 25 24 23 22 21   1 2 3 4 5 6 7 8 9 10 11 12

I set out to write a book about professional development and ended up writing a book about seeing—seeing the excellence around us and new possibilities for ourselves. Seeing and uplifting one another, our schools, and our profession.

This book is dedicated to my former colleagues.

I see you.

The PD Curator

HOW TO **DESIGN** PEER-TO-PEER **PROFESSIONAL LEARNING** THAT **ELEVATES TEACHERS** AND **TEACHING**

Acknowledgments

I want to thank the following people:

The staff at *Independent School* magazine, for publishing my articles about in-house PD and their questions during the editorial process that pushed my thinking forward.

Alecia Berman-Dry, director of outreach and professional development at the Association of Independent Maryland & DC Schools, for suggesting that I do a workshop on the topic of peer-to-peer professional development.

Participants at all my workshops on this topic, especially those early ones when I was still working the kinks out of the protocols.

My good friend Laurie Hornik, whose brilliance as both a teacher and an artist made me think of the curator metaphor that runs through this book.

Melanie Greenup, for being *that* mentor who looked at my sparks and saw fire and gently, but persistently, fanned the flames.

Eric Baylin and his colleagues at the Packer Collegiate Facilitative Leadership Institute, for first introducing me to the idea of creating structured processes for colleagues to learn from one another.

The many educators working with the School Reform Initiative. The protocols in this book are original, but the idea of using protocols to create a framework for meaningful faculty learning is not. I am grateful to those whose efforts inspired mine.

Carley Moore, for teaching me that writing can be a way for teachers to discover and deepen their thinking about their practice.

My co-everything, Jonathan Weinstein, for introducing me to contextual behavioral science, nerding out with me about relational frame theory, coauthoring the protocols for students on which some of the protocols for teachers in this book are based, and—most importantly—being a loving partner.

My good friend Taslim Tharani, who listened to me talk and talk and talk about this work and who believes in it so much that she uses it in her own work. (If you knew Tas, you'd know that's high praise.)

Susan Hills and Jamie Greene, my editors at ASCD, for wallowing around with me in the concept, message, details, and structure of this book until they were right. Both Susan and Jamie patiently gave me a chance to work through a lot of bad ideas and drafts. If this book is any good, it's because of their wise guidance.

Jill Stoddard, Ryan Harrity, and Timothy Riley, for reading the manuscript (during the early days of the COVID-19 pandemic, no less) and providing thoughtful feedback.

My former teaching partners and collaborators—Lauren Keller, Dori Kamlet Klar, Melissa Teitel, Kalin Taylor, Rachel Gayer, Renee Charity Price, Eliza Alexander, Laurie Hornik, Corey Blay, Janet Goldschmidt, Dina Weinberg, Rochelle Reodica, and Mollie Sandberg—who generously provided their time and thinking so every day was a PD day.

My parents, Harold and Leslie, and my kids, Allison and Jason.

And my students. All of them. Always.

Introduction: A Case for Peer-to-Peer PD

My former colleague Sharan was one of those absolutely *brilliant* teachers, yet for a long time, I didn't know this from actually watching her teach. We didn't have a culture of peer observation (even though we wished we did). Sharan and I were discussing this one day, and we agreed that we would try to start a new trend of popping into one another's classrooms. A few mornings later, when she was teaching and I wasn't, I visited her.

I learned a ton. I thought my sense of pacing was good, but she managed to pack more learning into 45 minutes than I would have thought possible. Her students always began with what she called a cognitive warm-up (which I won't describe because I'm hoping she'll write her own book about it). Next, Sharan had her students write diary entries from the perspective of either Romeo or Juliet right after they met. Every student had actively participated in two different meaningful activities, and it was only 10 minutes into the period.

The diary entries also springboarded into the main lesson on foreshadowing. Sharan's students defined *foreshadowing* in their own words, offered examples of foreshadowing from *Romeo and Juliet,* and then read the prologue to Act II. Her students quickly pushed their desks against the walls, formed a circle, and read the text several different ways to begin to understand its meaning. Sharan then had her students get into pairs, sit on the floor (where they'd been standing in a circle), and analyze the prologue. She also harkened back to the beginning of the lesson by asking how the prologue foreshadowed later developments in the act. By the time I was headed downstairs to teach my class, I'd taken five pages of notes.

One of the best ways to learn how to be a better teacher is by watching, listening to, and experimenting with the practices of great teachers. I started to think about other colleagues I could learn from. From Abena, I could learn how to raise the issue of justice from within the curriculum, ask appropriate questions, and push students to discuss them within a safe environment. From Vincent, I could learn how to use music to help students better understand the content—and more generally, how to create a stimulating atmosphere for learning. From Elizabeth, I could learn how to keep students focused on respecting their diverse thinking processes over finding a "right" answer. I also thought about what my colleagues could learn from observing me.

Meanwhile, our school was spending thousands of dollars a year sending teachers to conferences and institutes and bringing in high-priced consultants to tell us about the latest education fads. Sometimes these consultants gave us nothing but jargon and slideshows, and we were left wondering why their paychecks were so much larger than ours. But even when the presentations advanced our thinking and gave us clear takeaways, the message was still that *this person* was the expert . . . which meant *we,* the teachers, were not.

I don't want to sound ungrateful; lots of schools and districts make teachers fund their own whiteboard markers, so high-quality professional development (PD) is out of reach for far too many. It's important for teachers to stay current and not get so trapped in our own bubbles that we miss opportunities to learn from innovators outside our schools. But what about the innovators inside our schools? Why couldn't we learn from them?

I was lucky enough to have a department chair who encouraged teachers to learn from one another and created opportunities for us to learn together at our meetings. That was how I found out about some of Sharan's practices and why we originally ended up talking about observing each other. But then it was up to us to find time to visit each other's classrooms.

It was also up to us to keep our minds busy when we sat through speaker after speaker who talked about stuff that didn't directly relate to our experience or that we already knew—or that someone in the room could have presented better. No wonder so many of us spent those sessions texting, emailing, doodling, or whispering to one another. It's not especially respectful when teachers behave this way, but it's also understandable. Teachers have very little patience for PD sessions that lack relevance to their students and subject, when purportedly new information and strategies are just repackaged versions of the same old same old, when a high-priced consultant tells them what they already know and lacks interest in their own perspectives, or when they have no opportunities to generate and share ideas.

Right around the time I was noticing how much untapped talent my school had, I joined Twitter. There, I found a huge community of teachers who were actively seeking professional growth. I started participating in Twitter chats, which is when a large group of users discuss a predefined topic at a specific time, and quickly discovered there are chats on every topic imaginable—from assessment to game-based education to LGBTQIA+ equity. There are chats for teachers of every grade level and subject, and there are chats for teachers in specific states and districts. In every case, teachers use their "free time"—time that could be spent with their families or leisure pursuits—so they can learn not from an edu-celebrity but from one another. Why can't we also do this within the confines of the school day and with our own colleagues instead of with a bunch of internet strangers?

Twitter chats and rogue peer observation sessions are just two examples of teachers seeking more meaningful professional learning from and with one another. Other forms of peer-to-peer PD include edcamps, where participants just show up and share their expertise (Edcamp Foundation, n.d.); pineapple charts, which are ways teachers let colleagues know they're doing something cool and worth watching; #ObserveMe signs, which invite people into classrooms to offer feedback; and book clubs, which happen in person and online.

However, even though today's teachers have more choices than ever in what and how they learn, personalized PD creates its own set of problems. First, given a choice, people often gravitate toward what's familiar, easy, comfortable, or fun (Hayes, Strosahl, & Wilson, 1999; Waltz & Follette, 2009). Teachers might seek PD in the very areas in which they're already strong and avoid PD in the areas that would be most beneficial to them—out of a fear of exposing their weaknesses, a lack of interest (which contributed to their lack of skill in the first place), or a belief that they already know as much as they need to in a given area.

Second, just because teachers are the ones creating their own professional learning events doesn't mean those events are good. Just as there can be a boring, incoherent, and ultimately worthless keynote speaker, there can also be a boring, incoherent, and ultimately worthless edcamp session, Twitter chat, or book group. The events teachers create for themselves, or at least those they choose for themselves, won't necessarily include diverse perspectives or give everyone a way to contribute. Arguably, education consultants create better sessions simply because they have more practice and opportunities for participant feedback.

Finally, if each teacher goes off on his or her own personal PD journey, then there's no *shared* journey. Colleagues don't necessarily discuss their learning, learn together, or learn from one another. The learning events don't necessarily build on each other in an intentional way or change practice at the school level.

This book is about how professional learning experiences can become more inclusive, participatory, cohesive, and effective—and about the role you, as a leader, can play in creating those experiences. That role isn't so much administrative as it is *curatorial* —selecting content, creating a process for how people interact with it, fitting the pieces together into a meaningful whole, and discovering whether the event has been successful.

When I first started teaching, I'm not sure I'd ever used the word *curate*. I knew what it meant, but since I didn't work in a museum or the art world, I don't think I ever had occasion to say the word out loud.

Now, everybody is talking about curating. We curate our news feeds, our playlists, our weekends, and our sock collections. In this book, we'll explore what it might mean to curate professional learning.

Some professional curators lament the fact that *curate* has become a buzzword, used whenever anyone selects and assembles a bunch of stuff they like. They argue that curation is a more serious and demanding pursuit than picking out tapas for a dinner party or not-obnoxious people to follow on Instagram. They want to give the word *curate* back to museums, art, and artifacts. It seems like this gripe has less to do with which things can be curated and more to do with what the act of curation entails.

Although I'm not usually one to get excited about etymology, the word *curate* has a history that matters for purposes of this book. *Curate* comes from the Latin verb *curare,* meaning "to take care of." Curation is care. At a museum, curators care for the collection. They know about each photograph, gown, or fossil. They can tell you what an object is, point out details, and explain how it was found or made. They know how to preserve and protect it. They know how to display it so others can appreciate it. Increasingly, they care not just for the objects themselves but for the people who come to view, understand, admire, honor, interrogate, and learn from them.

Curators design ways for people to interact with objects and with one another, creating an immersive intellectual, emotional, and social experience—or at least the potential for one—while attending to people's needs. The artwork and artifacts, and the experience they contribute to, need to be accessible to and respectful of everyone. As a PD curator, you're not just giving teachers an exciting menu of options to choose from—or even weeding out the boring and pointless ones. You're caring for the professionals and for the profession.

Each chapter of this book includes practical tools and protocols you can use alone or in combination to help you become a curator of meaningful in-house professional learning. Along the way, we'll explore some of the psychology behind tapping into the expertise and interests of a diverse faculty, accounting for the vulnerability that peer-to-peer PD invokes, building professional learning units, and supporting teachers as they adopt and adapt new practices.

Chapter 1 discusses how to *structure* teachers' schedules to make time for in-house professional learning, along with how to set up their spaces to create a learning culture. Rather than encouraging large-scale changes, this chapter offers suggestions for how to use the resources you already have at your school.

Chapter 2 is about how to make professional learning *inclusive*. Just as museum curators can legitimize artists by including their work in a show, PD curators have the power to legitimize the work of diverse teachers and the entire teaching profession. Instead of only looking to "thought leaders" and hot topics for material worthy of study, you can discover talent inside your school building and deliberately elevate teachers' voices. The tools in this chapter are designed to help you build your awareness of faculty expertise, interests, goals, and needs, which you can then leverage in peer-to-peer PD.

Chapter 3 is about how to make professional learning *participatory*. Just as many museum curators don't simply display work but rather invite active engagement, PD curators can provide teachers with safe, authentic, and flexible ways to learn from and with one another. This chapter contains six ways to structure professional learning so teachers will find it relevant, dynamic, and enriching for their personal practice and relationships. Each of these professional learning structures includes a step-by-step process, reflection questions, and suggestions for how you can support teachers who use them.

Chapter 4 is about how to make professional learning *cohesive*. Good curation, whether of art, artifacts, or PD, involves more than selecting things that go together and pleasing the audience. It also involves designing a set of experiences that build on one another and move in a clear direction. This chapter shows how to create a meaningful professional learning series or unit so that instead of being one-and-done, each

PD event contributes to a larger outcome. The chapter discusses two kinds of PD units, gives examples, and explains how to create your own based on priorities at your school.

Chapter 5 is about how to make professional learning *effective*. For any curator, assessing how well the curated content worked depends on what we mean by *working*. This chapter offers three different definitions of what we might mean by effective PD and includes assessment tools based on each of those definitions.

Finally, whereas the first five chapters focus on how to curate professional learning, **Chapter 6** focuses on why that work might be worthwhile to *you*—even with everything else you have to do. It includes self-reflection exercises to help you bring your own values to the work of curating inclusive, participatory, cohesive, and effective PD.

Building Foundations for Professional Learning

When my daughter, Allison, was a toddler, my mother-in-law took us to the Museum of Modern Art in Manhattan. The photos from that outing make Allison look like an art connoisseur as she posed in front of different paintings. But, really, we zipped through the galleries since she had little interest in just looking at the art. I felt bad. We were at one of the greatest museums in the world, with seemingly all the time in the world, to see art that was there for the seeing, and my kid just wanted to go to the café. Still, even with her refusal to "do" the museum, she understood, as a toddler, what "doing" the museum would have meant. That's because the environment was arranged to encourage a very particular set of actions—looking at and lingering over paintings.

Museum curators are experts at arranging environments to influence how people relate to the things on display—and to one another. Art historian Svetlana Alpers (1991) calls that special way of focusing attention "the museum effect—turning all objects into works of art" (p. 26) and catalogs a dizzying number of decisions that exhibition designers make to create the museum effect:

> The way a picture or object is hung or placed—its frame or support, its position relative to the viewer (Is it high, low, or on a level? Can it be walked around or not? Can it be touched? Can one sit and view it or must one stand?), the light on it (Does one want constant light? Focused or diffuse? Should one let natural light and dark play on it and let the light change throughout the day and with the seasons?), and the other objects it is placed with and so compared to—all of these affect how we look and what we see. (Alpers, 1991, p. 31)

In other words, designing a museum exhibition is more than just putting art or artifacts on view; it's also about designing an environment that encourages a particular type of viewing.

School environments are not necessarily designed with adult learning in mind. (We might argue they're not even designed with children's learning in mind, but that's a topic for a different book.) No school I've ever visited has a room called "the professional learning center," and I've never seen a teacher's schedule that has a dedicated PD period.

Unlike museums that might devote an entire room to a single object and encourage visitors to spend as much time looking at it as they wish, time and space in schools are scarce. Even if you like the professional learning ideas presented in this book, you won't actually *use* them if you don't think you're set up to do so. Therefore, before we turn our attention to leading in-house professional learning, let's explore how to make time and space for it.

There's nothing I can do or say that will give you more hours in the day or more square footage in your building. Instead, this chapter will offer ways to help you use the time and space you *do* have for professional learning.

Making Time for Peer-to-Peer PD

When I started working at a school we'll call the Isidore Topial School, I was excited to learn that teachers met often in different configurations. In the middle school division, most of us taught four sections of the same course, which meant we had to prepare just one set of lessons and assignments. That freed up time to give more substantive feedback on student work, give extra help to students who needed or wanted it, talk to parents, and meet with one another.

Our weekly schedules included two grade-level team meetings during school hours. One was called "student review" because we discussed individual students about whom we had concerns, shared strategies that worked for them, and developed plans for supporting them further. The other meeting had no special title (although in the early years, it was called *nonstudent review*). At those meetings, we planned for our advisory periods, field trips, guest speakers, family conferences, and anything else we did as a grade level outside our academic classes. Over time, as those programs became more entrenched, we stopped feeling like we needed that second meeting and eventually discontinued it.

In addition to the grade-level meetings, we also had one weekly after-school meeting where the full faculty came together to hear presentations or have discussions in small groups. Occasionally, we met with our colleagues who taught the same subject at department meetings, the agendas for which department chairs had the autonomy to set. During these meetings, the group would make decisions (such as whether to order new materials), discuss schoolwide initiatives (such as how we planned to use a summer book within our content area), or plan for future instruction (such as how to teach about an upcoming election).

Topial also had two in-service days per year, which was when we could come together with teachers from the elementary and high school divisions (though we didn't always do that). Beyond attending these mandatory meetings, many teachers chose to meet in various configurations. For example, when I taught 6th grade English, I frequently met with the other 6th grade English teacher. I also volunteered for various committees and task forces.

Although Topial had an ideal structure for peer-to-peer professional learning, we rarely engaged in it during our meetings. Some team leaders and department chairs tried, but they either didn't do it often enough (or meet often enough) for the learning to feel routine, or they faced resistance because they were perceived as pushing their own agendas. If one 7th grade team leader asked her team to keep meeting twice a week to do PD together but another team leader only met once a week, it felt unfair. There were even teachers who approached our union reps to ask if they had to attend what they perceived as *extra* meetings when they were already going to so many—most of which felt unnecessary. Sometimes it seemed as if the only thing we did more often than go to meetings was complain about them!

There will always be people who simply don't want to do what they perceive as *more work*. For many of us, though, the issue was the meetings' content rather than their frequency. We attended *lots* of meetings to hear information that could have been relayed in emails. We talked about the same students repeatedly without changing our methods of intervention, let alone our curricula or pedagogies. We listened to out-of-touch guest speakers tell us things we already knew or that wouldn't work at our school. We listened to administrators blame and shame us without reflecting on their own practices—or worse, they offered vague praise without appreciating the excellence within our ranks. We listened to the same few white people pontificating. So many meetings were a waste of time at best.

At one point, frustrated by all those meetings, we (ironically) organized our own meeting to come up with better ways to use all that meeting time! We brainstormed topics we wanted to explore together. Although our principal told us we could form professional learning groups, he made attendance mandatory and the work itself directionless. That satisfied no one; those who thought there were already too many meetings felt like the learning groups just added to their workload, whereas those who wanted to do more purposeful PD felt like they were designed to appeal to the lowest common denominator and appease an angry faculty. In the end, our grassroots attempt at in-house PD faded away—like so many other initiatives.

For our purposes, we can learn two lessons from my former school's numerous meetings:

- **No matter how often teachers meet, it's important to prioritize peer-to-peer professional learning during those times.** That doesn't mean *every* meeting must be used that way, but the more time you devote to PD, the more actual learning you make possible—and the more meaningful those meetings feel.
- **If you want to do peer-to-peer professional learning, you need to build time for it into the schedule and calendar.** That doesn't mean the only way to do this work is the way my former school did, by having teachers meet three times per week, plus twice a year for in-service days. But the more time you allocate for teachers to meet with one another, the more time you have for PD.

Using Scheduled Meetings

If your school has in-service days or scheduled late starts, you can use those for in-house PD. You can also devote any full-faculty or departmental meeting time to professional learning. If you typically use meeting time to distribute information, you can send out that information in an email or video instead. (You might worry that some teachers won't read the email or watch the video, but the truth is that some teachers won't listen at a meeting either, and sending information digitally allows you to track clicks.) If teachers use meeting time to plan curriculum or programs, discuss individual students, analyze data patterns, or make decisions, then you might feel like there's no time left for peer-to-peer learning. In that case, you can make a values-based decision about whether it would be worthwhile to take time away from some of these important activities so teachers can learn from one another.

Arranging Substitute Coverage

Another option is to arrange substitute coverage for classes while teachers engage in professional learning together. If your school offers substitute coverage for teachers who attend offsite conferences, why not do the same when teachers attend in-house PD events? Odds are you won't be able to provide subs for the whole faculty at the same time, but most of the PD formats presented in this book occur in small groups, and these groups don't need to meet concurrently.

Creating Opt-In PD Events

Alternatively, teachers can meet after school or during summer break, in person or virtually, using an online meeting platform or social media chats. If you ask teachers to work outside their usual schedule, pay them for their time.

Structuring Teachers' Time

Figure 1.1 has a set of questions to help you reflect on how your school structures teachers' time beyond their contact hours with students. There is no right or wrong answer to any question. However, if any of your responses make you at all uncomfortable, notice that feeling, because it might mean you're out of alignment with your values.

At this point, maybe you feel like you could make the time for in-house professional learning—whether by using the meeting time you already have or by tweaking your schedule to create that time—but you have a feeling that your faculty isn't ready to use their time that way . . . or you can't convince the person who makes scheduling decisions to do this because *they* don't think it's going to work. That's because time is only one structural consideration that shapes what will and won't work in a school.

Orienting Teachers to Learning

Although museum visitors might quickly infer the rules of engagement—as Allison did at a very young age—they still need time to figure out which exhibits they want to visit, how long they'll stay in each one, how to get around the museum, and so on.

Professors John Falk and Lynn Dierking (2018) explain that first-time museum visitors behave differently than people who visit frequently: "Much of the first-time

---

FIGURE 1.1

Questions About Structuring Teachers' Time

- Which of the following does your school use?
  — During-school meetings
  — Before-school meetings
  — After-school meetings
  — Late starts
  — Early dismissals
  — In-service days
- In what configurations do teachers meet?
  — Full faculty
  — Subject-area departments
  — Grade-level teams
  — Interest groups (such as committees or task forces)
  — Professional cohorts (such as for new teachers)
- What is supposed to happen at these meetings? What actually happens?
- Do these meetings occur daily? Weekly? Monthly? A few times a year? Why that frequency?
- Could at least some of these meeting times be used for professional learning?
- How often *could* different types of meetings occur? Whose permission would you need to hold meetings more frequently?
- Is there ever resistance to teachers meeting? If so, where is that resistance coming from?
- Who creates teachers' schedules? Why that person or group?
- How does the person or group that creates teachers' schedules decide who's free at the same time? Are there, or could there be, periods when those who teach the same subject or grade level are available? If not, how might the teachers who *are* available at the same time form professional learning cohorts?
- What is the process for proposing changes to the schedule? For deciding on changes? For evaluating whether the changes had the desired impact?
- When was the last time the schedule was tweaked or overhauled? Why then?
- Do teachers call those times when they're not teaching free periods? Planning periods? Prep periods? Something else?
- What might happen if a period called *professional learning* appeared on teachers' schedules?

---

museum visitor's attention is absorbed in orientation, way-finding, behavior modeling, and general efforts to cope with novelty. The frequent museum visitor, by comparison, knows where they are going and how to behave; they are able to focus more on exhibitions than are first-time visitors" (p. 52).

Maybe you've witnessed similar "efforts to cope with novelty" when educators not used to learning together attempt to do so. Topial had four divisions—two lower schools, a middle school, and an upper school—but we hardly ever all met together. Even when meetings were on my division's campus, I wasn't used to being there for that purpose and with that group of people, so there was a sort of disorientation I had to get over. I wasn't sure where to sit because my familiar colleagues were spread throughout the room, interspersed with people I recognized but didn't know, with people I didn't even recognize, and with people I'd talked to in the past but whose names I'd forgotten. As a result, at least some of the mental energy I could have devoted to learning was spent searching for people I knew, observing how those I didn't know were reacting to the presentations, and looking for potential allies in my learning and work.

We know that people need time to figure out their surroundings and find their way. That's why many schools have an orientation for first-year students. Kindergartners might have a week of half-days so they can get used to their classroom and its routines—and so they can start getting acquainted with their teacher and classmates. Incoming high school students also have an orientation day so they can find their way around the building and meet their teachers before starting any academic work.

But even though we use the word *orientation* to refer to such events, it's more of a psychological process. We orient ourselves to our physical, temporal, and social contexts. That is, we get used to the building, schedule, and groups in which we find ourselves. It's not that we *can't* do any learning or work before we've gotten used to those surroundings; even first-time museum visitors look at, appreciate, and remember the art—but it's a different overall experience. If we want teachers to engage fully in peer-to-peer PD and get more out of it, then we might consider how we structure their day-to-day physical, temporal, and social contexts to orient them toward learning from and with one another.

Structuring Interactions to Promote Learning

Before I started working at Topial, I was at a place we'll call the Wile School. At Wile, we didn't have nearly as many meetings as we did at Topial, but teachers' time and spaces were structured in a way that encouraged more informal learning interactions.

Wile faculty members who taught in the same department shared an office. As a 6th and 7th grade history teacher, I had a desk in the humanities office. There was a math department office, a language department office, a science department office, a music department office, and so on. The space where I spent most of my nonteaching time was also the space where teachers of English, history, geography, writing, cultural studies, and other humanities courses spent *their* nonteaching time.

In the humanities office, each of us had a desk, along with shelves where we could store our materials. We also had a small conference room with a round table where we could have longer discussions if we needed quiet. The conference room was lined with books we could all use. Wile's departmental offices were set up as ideal spaces for us to talk about curricular alignment, pedagogical best practices, individual students' growth over time, ideas for projects, and culturally sustaining teaching—so that's what we did. Just as museums structure space for engagement with art, Wile structured space in ways that encouraged conversations about teaching and learning.

At Wile, most faculty meetings were by grade level. Precisely because we *didn't* share an office but shared students, we needed time to discuss their needs as individuals and to plan grade-level programming such as field trips, special events, assemblies, and our advisory program. We sometimes had department meetings; however, most conversations about curriculum and instruction occurred in our offices. It almost wasn't necessary for us to have formal meetings, because we were together so often.

I say *almost* because we weren't *all* together all the time. During any given period, some of us were teaching, meeting with students, or arranging our classrooms. Still, by virtue of spending so much time working near the people who taught the same subject as I did, I had many opportunities to talk about teaching with my peers—and to grow as a designer of learning experiences.

At Topial, I rarely had opportunities to discuss curriculum and instruction as a member of the English department unless I created those opportunities for myself. Faculty offices were grouped by grade level, not by academic department. As a 7th grade teacher, I had a desk in the 7th grade office. Our desks were around the perimeter, facing the walls, so we had our backs to one another when we worked. A small table where we might have worked collaboratively was in the middle of the room, so any conversations held there would have distracted colleagues who needed silence. As a result, the table quickly became a repository for lost items. There were no common bookshelves or materials—only places for our individual belongings.

Topial's 7th grade faculty office's overall setup encouraged large-group conversation, but what were those conversations about? We didn't share a common curriculum; rather, we shared students and a principal, so that was what we talked about. (More accurately, that was what we *complained* about.) One by one, most of my colleagues decided that they preferred to work in their own classrooms or the library because the faculty offices felt too negative or antisocial. More than one person called them *toxic*.

Looking back, I wish I had started a conversation about how faculty spaces were designed, how we used those spaces, and what changes we might have made. Even though I didn't have the power to make those changes, I could have proposed them and started the discussion. Changing the space would have been easier than changing our faculty culture, though, because once we associate a place with a particular purpose or set of behaviors, it's hard to relate differently to that space—or relate differently to one another within that space.

Still, the arrangement of a space tells us how to behave there. Just walk into any auditorium; the rows of seats facing a stage or screen tells you you're supposed to sit quietly while watching and listening to whatever is in front of you. Likewise, go into any museum and notice how its designers structured the environment to encourage a particular type of behavior: focused seeing.

Wile structured adult schedules and spaces to encourage teachers to learn from one another in informal interactions. So even though we didn't have many established meetings, we were primed for a peer-to-peer learning program because we were having a lot of those conversations anyway. Building the foundations for peer-to-peer learning isn't just about carving out time for it. It also involves thinking critically about how the school is set up to be a learning environment so the leap to more formalized in-house PD is as small as possible.

Figure 1.2 has a set of questions to help you consider how your school structures teachers' interactions in ways that might encourage (or discourage) peer-to-peer learning. Again, these questions don't have right or wrong answers, but notice any discomfort you feel as you respond, because that might be a signal that your school is not set up in a way that reflects your values.

Starting Small

By now, it might sound like I'm arguing that the only way to make peer-to-peer PD work is to redesign your school schedule and faculty workspaces. That's not the case. You might want to make small tweaks, but drastic overhauls aren't necessary—and often aren't possible.

If there's one message to take away from this chapter, it's this: *use what you have.* Use available time for professional learning. Set up existing spaces to encourage

---

FIGURE 1.2

Questions About Structuring Teachers' Interactions

- Where do teachers go when they're not teaching (assuming there's ever a time when they're not teaching)?
- What are those spaces called? The lounge? The break room? The office? Consider how the name of a space might send messages about what people do there. Is there a space you could rename the *professional learning center,* for example?
- Are those spaces for everyone, encouraging people to drift in and out as they need to, and to sit wherever they choose, or are people assigned to specific places?
- If teachers have dedicated offices or other places to go, how do they share those spaces? Is it by the grade level they teach? The subject? Is it random?
- Based on who shares a given space, what kinds of conversations are likely to occur? What kinds of conversations actually occur?
- How are adult spaces arranged? Are there individual desks? Small tables? How are these positioned relative to each other? Do teachers face one another?
- What resources are in those spaces? Is there a bookshelf with professional literature? A bulletin board with pictures or projects? A table where magazines the school subscribes to are laid out?
- How are those resources organized? Maintained? Kept up to date?
- What kinds of technology do teachers have access to? Does each teacher have a dedicated device or do they share?
- What digital tools encourage and enable colleagues to communicate with each other? Are all teachers trained in how to make full use of these tools? Who provides trainings? How often is training offered?

---

professional learning. Most importantly, just start *doing* professional learning with your faculty. You don't need to download a museum's app, preorder tickets, and look up all the works of art online to visit a museum; you can just go. Similarly, one of the best ways to build a foundation for in-house PD is to start doing in-house PD.

One event, or one group trying out the practices described in the upcoming chapters, is a start. Even using one strategy to determine what teachers want to learn about—or what they can contribute to one another's learning (which you'll hear much more about in the next chapter)—is a start. Taking one small step isn't just better than doing nothing; it begins orienting teachers to the fact that their professional environment is a learning environment.

Over time, you might find that you can do more. You might find that teachers who try in-house PD once ask to do it again. Or you might find that teachers who hear about colleagues in other departments learning from and with one another want their own departments to do it too. You might even find that teachers suggest ways to use time and space you haven't thought of. If teachers start asking for in-house PD, building it will still require work, but you might find that work more satisfying when you know your faculty cares about it as much as you do. You might even discover that some teachers are willing, if not eager, to share the workload.

Onward

This chapter asked you to consider how your school's systems and structures are already conducive to peer-to-peer learning, and what you might change to make it more conducive to that learning. It explored different ways to accommodate in-house PD within the school schedule and to orient teachers toward learning together. Ultimately, we saw that what's more important than making time and space is to use the time and space you have and just get started. In Chapter 2, we'll see *how* to get started by eliciting all teachers' expertise and learning goals.

Make It Inclusive:
Preparing for Professional Learning

As a child living near New York City in the late 1970s and early 1980s, I was lucky to have access to some of the world's greatest museums. My parents and grandparents took me to the American Museum of Natural History, where I saw dinosaur bones; the Metropolitan Museum of Art, where I'd imagine myself inside the suits of armor; and the Hayden Planetarium, where I'd stare up at projected constellations named after the Greek gods and goddesses I'd read about in my favorite book. I liked to write even then, so museums were opportunities for me to use my imagination and discover ideas I could put into my stories.

In all that seeing, I never considered what I *didn't* see—at least, not when I was a kid. I walked into a museum, and there was a painting, a sculpture, a skeleton, or an axe. I never thought about all the *other* art and artifacts that could have been on view but weren't. And I certainly didn't think about who selected the things I saw, why those people deemed these particular objects worthy of display, and what biases shaped their decisions. Nevertheless, whether or not we pay attention to it, curators—and the institutions that employ them—decide whose work sees the light of day, which pieces get displayed, how they're viewed, and, ultimately, what counts as *good* or *important*. Curation is an inherently political act.

Arts writer and former professor Maura Reilly (2018) uses the term *curatorial activism* to describe the imperative to show works by members of historically marginalized or minoritized groups. After explaining that despite "decades of postcolonial, feminist, antiracist, and queer activism and theorizing, the art world continues to exclude 'Other' artists—those who are women, of color, and LGBTQ" (p. 17), Reilly describes exhibitions that have given artists in these groups more visibility. She calls for acknowledging, resisting, and challenging bias in all its forms—by recognizing disparities and actively noticing and questioning our own internalized ideas of who should be included and why. That is, equality is not equity. Even if we treat everyone the same, our standards can reflect dominant ideologies and have disparate effects.

Education professor Lee Ann Bell (2008) makes a similar argument about teaching standards, prompted by a group of girls enthusiastically naming as their favorite teacher a Black woman that Bell—herself white—never considered to be especially good. It's not that Bell thought all Black teachers were inherently worse; it's that she had applied "an unconscious racialized lens" (p. 288) that saw "warmth and positive feedback as an essential way of engaging student voices and encouraging democratic participation" without considering "that there might be other ways of reaching these goals, or even that warmth could be expressed in various voice tones and at other volumes" (p. 287). Reflecting further, she explains, "As a white, middle-class person, I could take for granted that my definitions of good teaching would be supported by research, journals, and books created largely by people like me and, though grounded in our particular experiences, presented as universal truths" (p. 288).

From Reilly and Bell, we can learn that curatorial activists expand the definitions of *good teaching* to include those who have been marginalized within the field of professional learning. Teachers—as opposed to education authors and consultants—are already underrepresented in their own learning. When I think back on the conferences I've attended, I can't think of a single keynote speaker who had to get substitute coverage for their classroom so they could address us. And when I recall the people paid to deliver PD for in-service days at schools where I've taught, as well as the authors of books we bought for facultywide reads, the lists are overwhelmingly white. Only when the topic was related to diversity or equity did my schools bring in BIPOC (Black, Indigenous, and people of color) presenters and authors.

What about you? When you think back on the PD workshops and conferences you've attended, who were the presenters? What about the presenters at in-service days and the authors of schoolwide professional reads? As a leader, which presenters and authors have you sought out? Where did you look for them? How did you look for them? How do you determine what the teachers in your school want and need to study? How do you decide which PD providers, and which PD concerns, are worth including?

If our answers to these questions leave us feeling angry, disappointed, or defensive, that's a sign that something important to us is at stake. What might we do differently?

How can we, as PD curators, solicit teacher expertise and interests, using an expansive definition of *good teaching* and honoring voices beyond those we already hear?

In exploring some of the reasons for exclusion in the art world, Reilly (2018) asks if one problem is a knowledge deficit—curators simply don't know about artists beyond the straight white men whose work they've already seen or heard of—coupled with an unwillingness to educate themselves. As PD curators, we must do better. We can seek out expertise and learning goals within our schools, deliberately looking beyond our current knowledge base. But how?

If you want to find out what teachers know and can do, along with what they *want* to know and be able to do, you could simply visit their classrooms or ask them. But these methods of gathering information have limitations.

Limitations of Observing Teachers to Determine Their Expertise and Interests

One way to search for teacher expertise and learning goals is to spend more time in their spaces—especially those spaces with which we are less familiar and in which we might be uncomfortable. If, before you took on your leadership role, you were a history teacher, then consider spending time in the gym, art room, and science lab. If you took French in school, visit some Spanish classes; even if you don't understand the conversation, you can learn a lot about a teacher's practices from observing how students interact with the material and one another. If your past professional interactions have mostly been with members of a particular sociocultural group, look for ways to interact with and learn from members of other groups—taking care not to explicitly or implicitly ask them for their unpaid labor in educating you.

Putting yourself in unfamiliar teaching spaces might sound like a good idea, but don't you already have enough to do? Every administrator I've met says that even though they love spending time wherever teaching and learning occur, they have other responsibilities that keep them in their offices. If you're like most leaders, you already have a much-too-big job and limited time for walkthroughs.

Even if you could clone yourself and have your duplicate spend all day in classrooms, clone-you *still* wouldn't see all the expertise and learning needs that exist among your faculty. Classroom observation has at least five limitations:

- **We can only look at one thing at a time and, therefore, will only get a partial picture of what's happening in a classroom.** So much is going on in a classroom at any given moment that, even in a room with only 16 students and a teacher, there are at least 17 important places where you could look. In a traditionally run classroom where one person speaks at a time, you could look at the speaker, but then you'd miss interesting moments of listening, note taking, or silent exchanges of glances among everyone else—any of which might provide important information about the teacher's practice. Teachers who use small-group discussion protocols, writing-to-think activities, learning stations, student-driven inquiry, gamification, dramatization, or any other interactive learning strategy will provide you with all kinds of interesting dynamics and potentially useful information—that you'd miss if you were looking elsewhere. Additionally, great teachers do different things on different days (and even within the same period). Whatever we look at, we're missing something else.

- **What happens in the classroom is only a partial picture of a teacher's work.** Just as one painting doesn't show us the full scope of an artist's work, a single lesson doesn't give us a sense of whether students are having a singular experience or if they routinely engage in this type of activity, or how the lesson functions within a larger unit. Moreover, classroom instruction represents only part of what teachers do. Teachers also design lessons and units, write assignments and rubrics, make handouts and slideshows, give in-person and written feedback, engage in one-on-one conversations with students and their family members, display student work on walls and online, and configure their physical and virtual spaces. These processes and products might not be visible during a classroom visit.

- **Teachers might not have an opportunity to make certain kinds of expertise visible in their work.** A former colleague, Dina, was a substitute teacher for years before she was hired to teach English full time. In addition to being an excellent sub and English teacher, Dina was making art, getting certified as a yoga instructor, and starting a community garden. Through the sum of these experiences, Dina gained a unique set of skills and strengths that informed her work as an English teacher—not only because she occasionally had her students breathe mindfully or create a Shakespeare mural, but also because she approached everything (including her teaching) as an artist, yogini, and gardener. Her colleagues might have learned a lot from Dina if she'd had a chance to share her expertise in these areas. Walking through any teacher's classroom might not afford you the opportunity to see the full extent of their potential contributions.

- **Teachers' roles can shape our perceptions of their work.** Even if a teacher has opportunities to demonstrate a wide range of skills and strengths, we might so powerfully associate teachers with their roles that we don't see them as experts in anything else. When Dina began teaching English after having served as a substitute teacher, some people didn't take her as seriously as an English teacher as they took me, because they'd always known me as an English teacher—never mind that I'd previously taught history and had just as much experience teaching English when I started as Dina did. In my colleagues' minds, I was an English teacher and Dina was a sub. My role as an English teacher limited my colleagues' view of me. I wasn't seen as a curriculum design expert, even though I was good at it, wrote books about it, and gave workshops on it for teachers at other schools. Within my own school, I was seen strictly as an English teacher.
- **We might miss or misinterpret things that fall outside our expectations.** Maybe you've heard the adage, "We don't see things as they are; we see them as we are." We notice what matters to us, and we discount what doesn't. One time, when my principal observed me, I was teaching about literary imagery. I explained to my students that to engage their reader in an argument or story, they needed to create concrete and specific images, and that to create an image, they needed a concrete and specific noun—some *thing* for the reader to visualize. I then had them highlight nouns in the essays they were writing, look for places that were less noun-dense, and try adding imagery to those places. When I ran into my principal a few days later, I asked what she thought of the lesson. She replied, "The one about nouns?" Although I said yes, the lesson wasn't, in my mind, about nouns; it was about the power of imagery to engage a reader and using a revision strategy to add imagery to writing. My principal, however, viewed it as a grammar lesson and barely noticed the writing instruction.

Often, our attentional filters work to our advantage (I'd never have finished this book if I hadn't been able to tune out hallway noise and that ache in my shoulder). However, when observing teachers, that attentional filter has costs. We might not notice practices that matter most to the teacher—and for students' learning. Moreover, when we don't promote better ways of teaching because we don't see them right in front of us, and when we don't address certain learning needs because we think they're irrelevant, our students are the ones who suffer.

Limitations of Asking Teachers About Their Expertise and Interests

Another way to find out about teacher expertise and goals is to simply . . . ask. Instead of trying to be everywhere all the time, you can rely on teachers to see what's happening in their own classrooms, recognize excellence in themselves, and notice their individual and collective needs.

However, asking teachers to self-identify as experts—and as learners—presents its own set of problems:

- **Some of the best teachers don't see their practices as special or important.** Kelly, a former colleague, finds brilliantly creative ways to engage her students. On the first day of each unit, she dresses up in a costume to represent the content. (She has a Gregor Mendel costume, complete with peas, for her genetics unit, and to kick off learning cell biology, she dresses up as "Kel the Cell.") Kelly also uses humor to make the content more relatable. For a lesson on Punnett squares, instead of using the usual flowers and fruit flies, Kelly had students use emojis, assigning traits such as eyebrows and smiles as dominant, codominant, or recessive. Her costumes and funny assignments stimulate students' natural curiosity so their questions can propel the unit. "What's that thing?" a student might ask, pointing to the Golgi apparatus on her costume, or "What's up with the peas?" or "What traits are dominant in real life?"

    Kelly's creativity, courage, sense of humor, and love for her students are matched only by her humility. When I told her how brilliant her unit-opening costumes were, she just smiled and said the kids like them. When I told her how great the emoji assignment was, she was quick to tell me she hadn't made it up. (The fact that she didn't invent the technique doesn't mean she isn't an expert on how to use it or how to make new topics more accessible.) If the principal sent out a call for peer-to-peer PD proposals, Kelly *might* respond. She might, however, decline the opportunity to share practices she thinks of as "just the way I teach" or "something cool I found online." Just asking for expertise won't root it out if teachers don't see themselves as especially strong.

- **Teachers might not think of themselves as good at something if they can point to someone else they consider better at it.** I remember one time at a Passover Seder, we were all enjoying the festival meal and my mother-in-law showered my mother with compliments about the delicious food. My mother politely thanked her but quickly added, "I'm not the cook in the family; Lauren is." I might be more adventurous in the kitchen, but does that make me a *better* cook than my mother, whose fluffy matzoh balls and fork-tender brisket delight us year after year? And, more importantly, should my mother discount her own culinary skills just because she considers me to be a better cook? Too often, we define our expertise and strengths in relation to others—and find ourselves lacking. Asking teachers to name their strengths might only elicit self-judgment, and some of your most skilled teachers might not self-identify as experts because they can think of others they feel are better at certain things than they are.

- **Teachers might not notice strengths they don't associate with their jobs.** If a school administrator asked teachers to name their strengths, a science teacher might only consider how good she is at teaching students to ask questions, make observations, design experiments, and use other science skills. She might also notice strengths in teaching study skills, such as taking notes and making review guides, but she might *not* notice that she plans excellent field trips. My former colleague Shannon, another science teacher, is nothing short of masterful at planning field trips—she organizes students into thoughtful groupings based on their interests and needs, creates clear maps and schedules so chaperones know where to go and when, and balances structured hands-on activities with unstructured exploration and downtime for students to rest, play, and socialize. If Shannon were sent a survey that asked her to identify her teaching strengths or areas of expertise, she might not think to write "organizing field trips" because even though the trips connect to the science curriculum, organizing field trips is neither part of her job description nor measured on her evaluations. Therefore, she might not view it as the sort of contribution her colleagues would benefit from understanding. Just as leaders might so strongly associate teachers with their roles that they ignore expertise that falls outside those roles, so might teachers ignore expertise in themselves when it seems irrelevant or tangential to their primary job.

- **Even if teachers are aware of their strengths, they might not share them for fear of how they might look to others.** Teachers might worry about coming off as arrogant or about disappointing people—including themselves—if it turns out they have less to contribute than they'd thought. Worse, they might avoid sharing because they think they have great ideas that won't be appreciated by their colleagues or that their colleagues *will* appreciate their ideas but then apply them poorly and without giving credit.

We are sometimes our own worst judges. Asking teachers to identify their weaknesses, goals, or needs can be just as problematic as asking about their strengths—for similar reasons. Teachers might not see their own shortcomings. They might not think of themselves as *bad* at something if they can find someone else who's *worse*. They might not recognize weaknesses in areas they don't consider essential to their jobs. Even if they do recognize their needs, they might be afraid to share them with others for fear of seeming incompetent or of reinforcing someone's existing bias about them.

Eliciting Teachers' Expertise and Learning Goals

If we want to find out what teachers know and can do—along with what they want to know and be able to do—then we need processes that will help them recognize and share their own strengths and goals. The remainder of this chapter describes tools that empower teachers to discover their own expertise and learning needs and to share these in a way that feels safe.

The tools—Deictic Questions, Significant Moments in My Life as an Educator, Secret Appreciators, Core Values Assessment, Knowledge Discovery, and Growth Tracker—differ from one another in several ways (see Figure 2.1). Use whichever tool (or tools) you think would best serve your purposes and faculty.

How safe teachers will feel depends on your relationship with each of them, your relationship with the faculty as a whole, teachers' relationships with one another, status markers (such as how long they've been at the school and their standing as an employee), dynamics related to social identifiers such as race and gender, their personal and professional histories, and a host of other factors. Still, you shouldn't wait until after you iron out all the wrinkles from your faculty culture to start eliciting expertise and learning goals from teachers. In fact, just seeking this information, taking it seriously, and using it to build peer-to-peer professional learning experiences might help *create* a safer and more inclusive culture.

FIGURE 2.1
Tools to Elicit Teachers' Strengths and Needs

	Identify		Based On		Within		Through	
	Expertise	Learning Goals	Teacher Concerns	School Priorities	Oneself	One's Colleagues	Individual Reflection	Collaborative Discussion
Deictic Questions	●	●	●		●		●	
Significant Moments in My Life as an Educator	●	●	●		●		●	●
Secret Appreciators	●		●			●	●	
Core Values Assessment	●			●	●	●	●	
Knowledge Discovery	●			●	●		●	●
Growth Tracker	●	●		●	●		●	

Deictic Questions

This tool helps you design a questionnaire that expands teachers' awareness of their own strengths and learning needs by shifting their psychological perspective. Before we explore how to use the tool, let's first define what we mean by *psychological perspective*.

Throughout our lives, we experience everything as the person we call *I,* at a point in time we call *now,* and in a place we call *here* (Barnes-Holmes, Hayes, & Dymond, 2001).

These three words—*I, here,* and *now*—are speaker-defined. That is, each of us is referring to different people when we say *I,* different places when we say *here,* and different times when we say *now.* The word *deictic* comes from a Greek word for *perspective,* and deictic words such as *I, here,* and *now* depend on the perspective of the person using them.

Psychologists sometimes use the compound *I-here-now* to refer to a person's perspective (Foody, Barnes-Holmes, & Barnes-Holmes, 2012; Luciano, Valdiva-Salas, & Ruiz, 2012; McHugh, Stewart, & Almada, 2019), because we're always ourselves, in a particular place, at the present moment. Here's where it gets complicated. Precisely because we understand ourselves as *I,* that *I* implies the existence of other selves, whom we might call *you* or *he* or *she* or *they.* Because we understand the existence of a *here,* we also understand the existence of other places, both real and imaginary, which we refer to as *there.* And because we understand the existence of *now,* we can think of other times in the past and future, which we call *then* (Barnes-Holmes et al., 2001). *I-here-now* is my perspective, but *they, there,* and *then* refer to other perspectives that are not mine.

Because perspective has three components—*I, here,* and *now*—we can take other perspectives beyond our own by imaginatively shifting one, two, or all three of these components. That is, in addition to actually being *I-here-now,* we can imagine being *I-there-now* (ourselves at this moment, in another place), *I-here-then* (ourselves in this place, in the past or future), *they-here-now* (someone else in this place and at this time), *I-there-then* (ourselves in the past, in another place), *they-there-now* (someone else at this moment, in another place), *they-here-then* (someone else in this place, in the past or future), and *they-there-then* (someone else in the past or future, in another place). We might call these different perspectives (including *I-here-now*) the eight deictic variations.

How does any of this relate to curating professional learning? If we ask teachers to notice what they need from PD and what they can contribute to it, they'll approach the issue from the perspective of *I-here-now.* But if we ask them to consider their teaching from other perspectives, they might notice more aspects of their work than what they perceive as themselves, wherever they are at that moment. Figures 2.2 and 2.3 present questions that represent the eight deictic variations and are designed to elicit both faculty expertise (Figure 2.2) and faculty needs (Figure 2.3).

As it would be overwhelming for teachers to answer 16 questions in a single questionnaire, try choosing just a few—perhaps three questions from one figure or two questions from one figure and the two corresponding questions from the other. For example, you might send out a survey to your faculty that includes the following four questions:

FIGURE 2.2	
Questions to Elicit Faculty Expertise	
Deictic Variation	Example Question
I / here / now	When you look around your space or at your work, what brings you a feeling of joy, excitement, or satisfaction?
I / **there** / now	If you were presenting at a conference today, what would your session title be?
I / here / **then**	What about your space or work is better than it was a few months or years ago?
they / there / now	If visitors were in your room or looking at your work today, what do you hope they'd notice and perhaps ask about?
I / **there** / **then**	If you were moving and had to apply for a new job at a different school, what's a practice you'd hope to bring with you?
they / **there** / now	Imagine that right now, a former student is using something they learned from or got out of your class. What is it?
they / here / **then**	Think of something a student did that pleasantly surprised you. What did you do that might have helped lead to this student's action?
they / **there** / **then**	Imagine your students (or the students you serve) at their 25-year reunion. What do you hope they will say about their experience with you?

Source: Copyright 2021 by Lauren Porosoff.

FIGURE 2.3

Questions to Elicit Faculty Needs

Deictic Variation	Question
I · **here** · **now**	When you look around your space or at your work, what brings you a feeling of worry, frustration, or dissatisfaction?
I · **there** · **now**	If you were at a conference today, what would be the title of the session you'd most want to attend?
I · **here** · **then**	What about your space or work do you hope will be even better a few months or years from now?
they · **here** · **now**	If visitors were in your room or looking at your work today, what would you want them to ignore or forgive?
I · **there** · **then**	If you were moving and had to apply for a new job at a different school, what's a practice you'd hope to leave behind?
they · **there** · **now**	Imagine that right now a former student is relieved that they're *not* doing something they used to do with you. What is it?
they · **here** · **then**	Think of something your student did that unpleasantly surprised you. What did you do—even unintentionally—that might have helped lead to this student's action?
they · **there** · **then**	Imagine your students (or the students you serve) at their 25-year reunion. What do you fear they will say about their experience with you?

Source: Copyright 2021 by Lauren Porosoff.

- If visitors observed your lesson today, what do you hope they'd notice and perhaps ask you about?
- If visitors had been in your room today, what do you hope they would have missed or ignored?
- What about today's lesson was better than similar lessons you have taught in the past?
- When you teach similar lessons in the future, what do you hope will improve?

Note that the questions are worded slightly differently than those in Figures 2.2 and 2.3. Feel free to change the wording so the questions work better for your faculty. Alternatively, make up your own questions that use deictic variations to help teachers view their work from other perspectives and see things they might not otherwise notice. Also, you don't necessarily have to send these questions out in a survey. You might ask such questions in one-on-one meetings or even in casual interactions with teachers when you see them in the hallway, lunchroom, or lounge. You'll probably use less formal language in those cases!

When asking about strengths (using questions such as those in Figure 2.2), teachers will have to put their names on their surveys so you can tap them to share their expertise with their colleagues. However, when asking teachers to describe their shortcomings (using questions such as those in Figure 2.3), consider making the surveys anonymous, thus enabling teachers to feel safer opening up. You can use this information to design PD that meets your faculty's needs without invoking the shame and defensiveness that might result from asking teachers to disclose their weaknesses. Although you might eventually need to know who has which needs so you can address them with the appropriate individuals, Deictic Questions is designed to help you discover larger patterns within the community.

Significant Moments in My Life as an Educator

Whereas Deictic Questions has teachers shift perspective in a variety of ways, this tool has teachers use their present-moment perspective to look at their past. And whereas Deictic Questions has teachers reflect privately, the following activity has teachers discuss their significant moments with partners. In the intimacy of a one-on-one conversation, teachers can discover common experiences, interests, and values.

Rather than asking teachers directly about their strengths and weaknesses, Significant Moments in My Life as an Educator has teachers list moments that mattered to them in some way, create timelines of their five or six most significant moments, use those moments to connect with a colleague, and discover strengths and goals in themselves and one another—which might then help you build professional learning experiences for the whole group. Figure 2.4 presents some significant moments in my life as an educator, written on sticky notes and arranged in roughly chronological order.

This activity, adapted from the "Learning Timeline" exercise in *Teach Meaningful* (Porosoff, 2020), works well with groups of any size—from a small department to a large faculty. You'll need to bring enough sticky notes so each person will get six. Teachers will also need to bring their own writing materials.

FIGURE 2.4

Sample Significant Moments Timeline

1. Have teachers take out their writing materials. Explain to the group that they're about to do some reflective writing. They will not share anything they want to keep private and will share what they wish with only one person.

2. Ask teachers to list some of the most significant moments in their lives as educators.

3. As teachers make their lists, ask about a dozen of the following questions, two or three at a time. Asking two or three questions at a time allows teachers to focus on each one without feeling overwhelmed, and if they don't have an answer to a particular question, they can answer another one. Explain that the questions are intended to help them think of moments in their lives as educators that they find significant but that the prompts are meant to help—not limit—them. Teachers should feel free to skip questions, list multiple answers to any question, or ignore the questions entirely and just continue to list significant moments. Write the questions on a whiteboard or prepare slides with two or three questions per slide.

—What lesson or assignment got your students to do great things?

—What lesson or assignment did you drop from your course?

—When did you challenge your students?

—When did your students challenge you?

—When did you surprise your students?

—When did your students surprise you?

—What has a colleague done that inspired you to do something similar? (Name the colleague if you wish to.)

—What has a colleague done that inspired you to do the exact opposite? (Don't name the colleague.)

—When did you struggle to teach something?

—When did you have fun while teaching?

—What book, workshop, or conference transformed your practice?

—Who has mentored you, formally or informally, and what was the effect on your practice? (Name the person if you wish to.)

—Who has stood in your way professionally (or tried to), and what was the effect? (Don't name the person.)

—What's a time when you took good care of someone at school?

—What's a time when someone took good care of you at school?

—What's a time when you took good care of yourself at school?

—Which teaching day do you hope you'll remember forever?

—Which teaching day do you wish you could forget?

—What was a conversation with a student, parent/guardian, or colleague that went especially well?

—What was a conversation with a student, parent/guardian, or colleague that went especially badly?

—What has been said about you that you're glad is true?

—What has been said about you that you know is true but wish wasn't?

—What was the hardest you ever worked on a unit?

—What was the hardest you ever worked for a student?

—What are some of the biggest changes in your everyday teaching since the time you started?

—What's something you stopped doing in your teaching?

—What's something you've thought about trying in your classroom but haven't done yet?

4. Ask teachers to identify five to six of their most important teaching moments and write each one on its own sticky note. Then have them put those notes in roughly chronological order and share their resulting timelines with a partner.

5. As partners continue to talk, give or post the following questions to encourage further reflection. Partners may wish to move their timelines to where they can see both so they can think about them together.

   —What does meaningful teaching look like for each of us?

   —What are some key differences in our meaningful teaching experiences?

   —Even with the differences between us, what are some key similarities in how we define *meaningful teaching?*

6. Debrief the experience with the full group by giving the following prompts one at a time. As teachers share, listen for potential expertise and learning goals, and write them down.

   —What did you notice?

   —What kinds of teaching moments are meaningful to you?

   —What kinds of teaching moments do you want to share with others?

   —What kinds of teaching moments do you want to learn about from others?

Because this activity doesn't ask directly about expertise or learning goals, you'll need to listen intently for them. Circulate while partners have their discussions, and take notes during the debrief. Since not everyone will have a chance to share or feel comfortable doing so, you can also send a quick follow-up survey, using the last two questions from the debrief (*What kinds of teaching moments do you want to share with others? What kinds of teaching moments do you want to learn about from others?*). If nothing else, this activity might help you pay more attention to teachers who hadn't stood out to you before and consider how to include them when you design professional learning experiences.

Secret Appreciators

The previous two tools elicit teacher strengths and needs in a roundabout way, but this one directly asks what teachers are good at. However, instead of asking teachers to notice and name their own strengths, they notice and name their colleagues' strengths.

For Secret Appreciators, teachers fill out a slip that asks them to describe a colleague's strength (see Figure 2.5 for a sample appreciation slip). You could put the questions into an online form that you send out periodically. If you use paper forms, you can leave them in a common area so—as teachers wait for their coffee or copies—they might think about their colleagues' skills. You could also hand out appreciation slips at the end of a faculty meeting, when everyone can look around the room and perhaps recall something great they saw or heard about.

Although it would be faster and easier just to state someone's strength, the slip also asks teachers to describe their colleague's practice and its impact. A teacher wouldn't, for example, be able to simply write, "Jason is good at holding students accountable." What does that mean? What does it look like? What does Jason do? Why does it matter?

When teachers have to describe a colleague's practice, they can't simply give shout-outs to people they like or use jargon they've heard, such as "Claudine is good at SEL" or "Marc is good at culturally responsive teaching." As soon as terms like these become popular, people develop their own understandings of what they mean and sometimes use them in ways their originators never intended.

FIGURE 2.5

Sample Appreciation Slip

_____ is good at _____.

What makes you say so? Describe what this person does.

Why do these actions matter? What impact do they have on learning, work, or relationships?

Most of all, when teachers describe a colleague's practice, *you* can visualize exactly what the faculty member does—and potentially investigate further. A statement such as "Andre is good at getting kids to be creative" tells you that *something* cool is happening in Andre's classroom, but it doesn't tell you what. Are his students writing fairytales about integers, are they coming up with their own ways of solving problems involving integers, or are they making up their own problems? Any of these practices might be worth sharing, but without a description, you don't know. If you told Andre that you'd love to hear more about how he gets students to be creative, he might not know what prompted his colleague to say that about him, or his definition of *creativity* might be different from his colleague's.

The final question on the appreciation slip asks teachers to share impacts. Some practices might be fun or trendy, or they might look cute in a photo, but have little pedagogical value. Other practices, although they might not sound especially exciting in a description, might have a tremendous effect on student learning, work, or relationships. Asking teachers to describe these effects reminds them that impact matters and helps you see how a practice you might have discounted or misunderstood (or just didn't notice) is important in ways you didn't realize.

After you've read teachers' responses, you can pass them along to the faculty members they're about. Alternatively, you could read them out loud in faculty meetings as a way to recognize great teachers. However, keep in mind that doing this might make some teachers wonder why they haven't also been recognized. Over time, you might find that teachers fill out appreciation slips about colleagues who have not yet been recognized, and you can keep encouraging your faculty to fill out slips if they know of colleagues whose practices should be appreciated.

Core Values Assessment

Some schools and districts adopt a set of core values that articulate what matters to the community. For example, Mankato Area Public Schools (n.d.) in Minnesota have seven core values—integrity, respect, excellence, adaptability, responsibility, engagement, and collaboration. Thompson Falls Public Schools (2013) in Montana have five— excellence, unity, compassion, respect, and integrity. Though many schools use abstract qualities such as *integrity* and *compassion* to describe their core values, some schools and districts use verbs, such as the nine core values—empower, inspire, motivate, collaborate, nurture, respect, contribute, embrace, and partner—of Dennis-Yarmouth Regional School District (n.d.) in Massachusetts. Ellington High School in Connecticut expresses its core values as roles its students will take on—those of critical thinkers, innovators, honorable individuals, collaborators, and communicators (Ellington Public Schools, 2016).

If your school or district has a set of core values, you can look for two ways teachers make them manifest. First, you can look for how teachers bring these values to their *own* actions. For example, you might ask how teachers demonstrate adaptability, or how they nurture students, or how they express kindness. You can also look for ways in which teachers create a context for *students* to manifest the core values. For example, you might ask how teachers foster adaptability in their students, teach students to nurture one another, or evoke student kindness.

Core Values Assessment helps you determine potential sources of expertise in enacting the values your community has claimed for itself. Teachers receive a list of the school's core values along with two questions:

- Which of your colleagues enacts this value?
- Which of your colleagues creates opportunities for students to enact this value?

The survey also has a place for teachers to add comments so they can expand on anything they wrote. Figure 2.6 presents a core values survey form you could give out to faculty members (after you fill out the first column with your school's core values). You could also create an online survey with the same questions, which would make it easier for you to analyze the results.

When you receive the completed surveys, look for patterns. Which names come up repeatedly for a particular core value? These might be people worth tapping when designing PD around that value. For example, if several teachers say Mr. Torres creates opportunities for students to show empathy, perhaps his principal could ask him to share his knowledge during a professional learning event. You might also see certain names coming up across multiple categories; these might be teachers worth observing or talking to so you can better understand their skills and strengths.

However, only looking for the names that come up repeatedly might just lead you back to the people you already see as excellent. Therefore, when reviewing the survey results, also look for names that surprise you. Maybe they're the hidden gems within your school, and maybe they have knowledge worth sharing. These might be the people worth a closer look, whether that means a classroom observation, a visit to their website, or a one-on-one meeting.

If anything on a particular survey surprises you, consider talking to the person who filled it out, as they might define the core values differently than you do or be attuned to great ways of teaching that you don't notice. He, she, or they might have a perspective worth including when you're designing professional learning.

FIGURE 2.6

Core Values Survey Form

Your name:

Core Value	Which of your colleagues enacts this value?	Which of your colleagues creates opportunities for students to enact this value?

Please use this space to explain any of your responses.

Knowledge Discovery

So far, we've seen tools that provide broad views of faculty strengths and needs. What if you've already decided on a topic for professional learning? How do you determine what teachers already know and are capable of in this area, along with what they might need from their learning experiences?

When teachers introduce a new topic to their students, they often begin by assessing prior knowledge, both so students can build on that knowledge and to generate curiosity. This tool is a way to begin professional learning by exploring what teachers already know about the topic.

For the activity, teachers first draw images they associate with the topic. Yes, draw! Even though teachers might feel comfortable asking their students to draw their knowledge about, say, the Great Depression or parabolas, you might feel slightly less comfortable asking teachers to draw their knowledge about, say, social-emotional learning or outdoor education. But the drawings have a purpose. In the teaching field, we use a lot of abstract terms such as *social-emotional learning* and *outdoor education*. Abstract terms, by definition, do not refer to concrete things we can see or point to. When asked to share what we know about such a topic, we might just use other abstract words we haven't yet defined (for example, "Social-emotional learning means understanding our thoughts, feelings, actions, and relationships"), or we might use the same abstract words to create circular definitions (for example, "Outdoor education is when you . . . um . . . educate outdoors"). But when we draw, we force ourselves to imagine something concrete and then bring that mental picture into the physical world.

After everyone has a chance to look at all the drawings, the group discusses repeating images, which might reveal collective understandings they can build on or assumptions they'll need to challenge. Imagine that when a group of teachers is asked to represent their knowledge about outdoor education, many people draw kids in forests. These drawings reveal the assumption that outdoor education must take place in a forest, and the group might need to learn about how any outdoor space can be used to educate about nature.

The group also discusses outlier images—those that come up only once, seem surprising, or stand out in another way. These outliers might reveal different or more nuanced ways of thinking about the topic, which suggests that the group might learn something important from the colleagues who drew them. Let's say, for example, that one image of *outdoor education* shows kids in a canoe. The person who drew it might have had a different set of experiences with outdoor education from the rest of the group and can share important insights, regardless of whether she ends up taking her students on a canoe trip. Or imagine that among all the drawings of forests, there's one that shows a student measuring a tree trunk. The teacher who drew this might have valuable ideas about how to use the outdoors when studying curricular content such as geometry.

When teachers explore their shared ideas and diverse perspectives, they can appreciate one another's potential contributions to their own learning and prepare to learn more together. Your job, besides leading the activity (or delegating that responsibility to someone else), is to listen for your faculty's learning needs and find knowledge resources within your building.

For this activity, which is adapted from the Represent and Respond protocol in *Two-for-One Teaching* (Porosoff & Weinstein, 2020), each teacher will need two sheets of unlined paper and a pen or marker.

1. Explain that, as faculty, you'll be learning more about [the topic you're about to study] and that the day's work will help the group begin exploring the topic together.

2. Ask teachers to make a simple drawing that shows the images, memories, or associations that come to mind when they hear [the topic being studied]. Allow no more than five minutes for this step; two is usually enough. Some teachers might feel anxious about drawing, and limiting the time shows it's meant to be an exploratory exercise—not an art project. Let them know it's okay to use stick figures and simple shapes.

3. Invite teachers to silently walk around the room and view one another's work without hearing explanations. The lack of a verbal explanation allows the visual images to speak for themselves.

4. As teachers continue to walk around the room, ask them to grab their second sheet of paper and fold it in half. On the left side, have them list repeating images or kinds of images. On the right side, have them list outliers—that is, images or ideas that only come up once, are surprising, or stand out in another way.

5. Lead a discussion, using the following prompts:
   —Read through your list of repeating images. What accounts for these similarities? Why are *these* the images we associate with [the topic being studied]?
   —What do the repeating images tell us about ourselves? What seems important to us as a group?

—Read through your list of outliers. What's interesting about them? How do they expand our understanding of what [the topic being studied] can be?

—What do the outliers tell us about the colleagues who created them? What could we potentially learn from these colleagues?

—What *don't* we know about [the topic being studied]? What questions do we have?

During the discussion, listen for potential experts who can share their knowledge, and follow up with them as you design PD for the group. Also listen for comments and questions that indicate possible learning needs, and write these down so you can reference them later when introducing PD events.

Growth Tracker

Sometimes, when we want teachers to gain a particular skill set, we try to create buy-in by exposing a lack of capacity in this area, as if to say, "Look how badly we need to learn this!" Imagine, for example, that a principal thinks her faculty needs to do a better job teaching executive function skills. To prove to potential naysayers that they need this PD, she arranges for teachers to take a quiz that will expose how little they know about executive functioning and performs a curriculum audit that will expose how little they do to teach executive functioning skills.

Although it might be true that teachers urgently need certain types of professional learning, showing teachers their own inadequacies won't necessarily motivate them to participate in that learning—and it could invoke resistance. Some teachers might say they lack certain skills because it's not their job to have them: "Of course I don't teach about executive functioning; that's what their life skills class is for." Other teachers might point to a different problem: "Before we can teach executive functioning skills, we need to change our schedule so we have more time for stuff like that." If this isn't the first time they've learned about a particular topic, they might express frustration: "Executive functioning again? Maybe this time we'll actually learn something useful." Naming deficits can lead to blame and shame while ignoring the strengths teachers bring to their work.

Instead of framing PD as the solution to a problem, we can instead frame it as part of a meaningful journey that teachers have already begun. The Growth Tracker tool has teachers explore how far they've already come in gaining a skill set. That way, when they engage in further professional learning, they aren't being asked to start something new or start over; they're building on work they've started already. They're not being asked to do someone else's work; they're continuing their own. And they're not hearing that they're deficient; they're getting affirmation that they're good and have a chance to get better.

During the activity, teachers first list ways they've improved in an area—say, teaching students to manage their time, tasks, materials, and relationships. Then they list ways they can continue to improve so their future selves are even better in this area than they are now. A middle school teacher's growth tracking chart is shown in Figure 2.7.

Making these charts serves two purposes. It helps teachers notice their growth and feel motivated to keep growing, and it makes *you* aware of the expertise teachers have already developed (based on what they write in column A) and the goals they have for themselves (based on what they write in column B). After the activity, you'll know who can contribute to their colleagues' learning and what the group wants to learn how to do.

For the activity, each teacher will need a pen and a copy of the Growth Tracker Graphic Organizer (see Figure 2.8). You can either write in the area of focus in advance or have teachers write it in themselves during the first step.

1. Hand out copies of the Growth Tracker Graphic Organizer. Explain to the group that they'll be thinking about their growth in a particular area of focus. If you haven't already filled it out, tell teachers what to write for the focus area at the top.

2. Direct the group's attention to the three circles on the graphic organizer, which mark points in the past, present, and future. Ask them to fill in the blank in the left circle with an amount of time during which they've seen meaningful change in the focus area and to fill in the blank in the right circle with an amount of time during which they expect to see further change. For many teachers, a five-year period is long enough to see change, although some participants might not have been teaching for that long and others might not expect to be teaching for another five years. Teachers should consider their years of experience and any watershed moments in their professional history—such as switching schools or grades, working with particular colleagues, teaching particular students, or anything else that made a difference.

FIGURE 2.7

Growth Tracking by a Middle School Teacher

Focus Area: Teaching students executive functioning—how to manage their time, tasks, materials, attention, emotions, and relationships

	A		NOW		B	
5 years ago			NOW			5 years from now

Column A (5 years ago → NOW):

Cuing students that I'm about to ask a question that they might have a strong reaction to and asking them to notice that reaction (instead of scolding them for blurting it out)

Asking students to estimate how long each chunk of a task will take instead of telling them how long it should take

Asking latecomers/late-starters to look around the room for cues about what's happening right now

Spending five minutes at the beginning of work periods setting goals

Spending five minutes at the end of project work periods helping students self-assess how it went

Column B (NOW → 5 years from now):

Instead of mandating the use of a planner, teaching students how to create a system for themselves that helps them keep track of their assignments

Helping students set goals related to learning instead of grade goals

Teaching students how to chunk larger tasks instead of breaking it into chunks for them

Helping students work independently in groups instead of dividing up their responsibilities myself

Helping students actively listen to each other instead of just waiting their turn to speak

3. Have teachers write in column A the ways they've grown or improved in the focus area between the time they identified in the past and now. Some teachers might be able to make this list easily, whereas others might need more prompting. Try asking more specific questions, pausing so teachers can reflect on and respond to each one. For example, if you were leading this activity with respect to executive functioning, you might ask questions such as the following:

—How do you teach materials management better than you used to?

—What have you learned about breaking down tasks for students or helping them break down tasks for themselves?

—What do you do to help students manage their emotional reactions in class?

4. Have teachers write in column B the ways they want to grow or improve in the focus area between now and the time they identified in the future. Again, some teachers might need more specific questions to help them think of what to write.

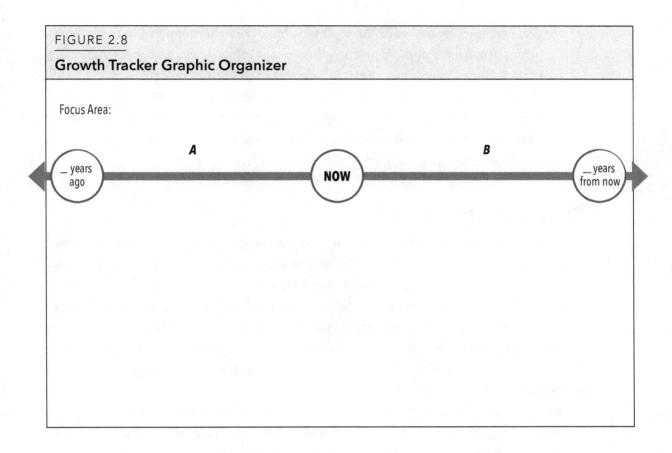

FIGURE 2.8

Growth Tracker Graphic Organizer

Focus Area:

The questions can be similar to those you asked about the past. For example, questions about executive functioning might include the following:

—How do you want your future self to teach materials management?

—How can you more effectively break down tasks for students or help them break down tasks for themselves?

—What do you want to be able to do to help students manage their emotional reactions in class?

5. Invite teachers to share anything they wrote or noticed while writing.

6. Offer three options for what to do with the papers. Teachers can submit papers with or without their names on them, or they can hold onto them. If the whole point of the activity is for you to find out what teachers know how to do and what they want to learn, the third option—allowing teachers to hold onto the papers—may seem counterintuitive. Remember, though, that the overarching

goal is to include the voices of those who have been marginalized in their own professional learning. Forcing people to share information before they're ready to do so doesn't empower them. *Inviting* them to share shows that you care about their ideas and think they can make an important contribution—and that you respect their autonomy enough to give them a choice about whether they share at all. If they want a voice in their own professional learning, handing in their papers is a preliminary way they can use that voice.

Toward Equity in Peer-to-Peer PD

We sometimes talk about diversity, equity, and inclusion as a single concept. We even have the acronym *DEI* to help us refer to the three ideas collectively. We can, however, have diversity without inclusion and inclusion without equity. That is, we can have a faculty that represents many different professional and cultural identifiers yet only bring certain people into conversations about professional learning (and into other conversations, too). We can give everyone a voice—which is what the tools in this chapter are designed to do—yet only acknowledge, respect, and heed what certain people say.

As you begin to curate professional learning, eliciting all teachers' expertise and needs is an important first step, but it's only a first step. We need to stay attentive to which voices we honor and privilege, which voices we dismiss or dispute, and what personal and structural biases might affect our ability to notice strengths and weaknesses in one another.

Onward

This chapter discussed ways to make professional learning more inclusive so diverse groups of teachers can contribute their knowledge, skills, interests, and goals. Because simply looking for or asking about teachers' strengths and weaknesses won't necessarily provide us with the information we're after, we can use perspective-taking tools to get that information. Once you've found out about teachers' expertise and needs, you can design PD that positions teachers as active participants in their own professional learning—and Chapter 3 offers lots of ways to do just that.

Make It Participatory: Structuring Professional Learning

When my daughter, Allison, was little, I took her to a newly opened children's museum that had lots of hands-on activities. She loved building, so I thought this would be an ideal experience for her. One station displayed intricate castles and bridges made from KEVA planks—precision-cut so that they could form stable and innovative structures. Nearby sat huge buckets of KEVA planks and tables where we could build. We were excited to start! However, Allison didn't know how to align the planks to produce different architectural shapes, nor did she have an image in her head of something she wanted to build. We puttered around for 10 minutes, arranging the planks into patterns without making anything satisfying, and then gave up.

In *The Participatory Museum,* designer Nina Simon (2010) imagines museums where visitors "actively engage as cultural participants, not passive consumers" (p. ii). Visitors might play quiz games, vote for favorite pieces of art, share personal stories related to an exhibit's theme, or—in what we hoped would be Allison's case—create their own compositions similar to ones they see.

The same is possible for PD. Instead of only *consuming* content—for example, by listening to an invited speaker on an in-service day, attending a conference, or reading an education book—teachers can engage more actively in their own professional learning and contribute to one another's learning.

But becoming an active participant, whether at a museum or a professional learning event, is more challenging than remaining a passive spectator. In museums, although spectators might read a placard or have a whispered conversation, their only real job is to look. Similarly, at many professional learning events, there might be occasional opportunities to ask questions or have a turn-and-talk, but all attendees really need to do is listen to the presenter. If we ask people to participate, they need to know *how*.

Spectators also don't risk anything. Walking around a museum and looking at art or sitting in a chair and listening to a presenter invokes no vulnerability. When we share ideas, tell stories, ask questions, analyze pieces of work, or create something new, we make ourselves vulnerable to other people's judgments and our own.

According to Simon (2010), museum visitors need a supportive starting point (p. 13) to help them participate meaningfully. Although the children's museum did a great job providing materials to explore, without a supportive starting point—models to replicate and strategies for how to build—even my engineering-oriented daughter felt overwhelmed, frustrated, and ultimately disappointed.

Let's think of this chapter's six formats for participatory professional learning—the workshop, the council, the exemplar study, the toolbox share, the intervision group, and the bringback—as supportive starting points that enable teachers to engage meaningfully with the material and one another.

The Workshop

A presenter has expertise in how to do something that's made a positive impact on students. The group experiences the practice, discusses what it would look like in their classrooms, and makes anything they need to implement it.

Suggested group size: 12–18

Suggested time: 45–90 minutes

In a workshop, an expert, or a small group of experts, presents to an audience of learners. Imagine that Wade, an 11th grade math teacher, has learned the flipped classroom technique (Bergmann & Sams, 2012). He makes videos in which he explains concepts and demonstrates problem-solving strategies. His students watch the videos at home, where they can learn at their own pace and then use their class time to solve problems collaboratively and discuss their processes. Wade has experimented with different ways of making, editing, and distributing the videos. He's figured out what to do when a student doesn't watch the video for homework, how to spot students who missed or misunderstood key points, and how to help students work together effectively. If his colleagues want to learn new ways to personalize instruction, promote critical thinking and creative problem solving, and teach collaboration skills, they don't need an out-sider. They have Wade.

Imagine that at a faculty meeting, Wade shows a video about how to flip classrooms. In his PD video, Wade explains his process for making and using math videos, describes some of his mistakes and challenges, shares student and parent feedback, and reflects on how this teaching method has influenced student learning. In groups, Wade's colleagues discuss what they noticed and come up with ideas for how they could flip their own classrooms. Then, during the next meeting, everyone tries making videos about their content while Wade circulates and answers questions.

Now imagine the results: A science teacher films a lab demonstration for her students to watch at home, thus gaining class time to ask questions and perform the lab. A group of English teachers turns a slideshow about using textual evidence into a video that students can watch before writing essays. Even though not all teachers end up using the videos, they've all learned the skill and had an opportunity to think about how they encourage deep and collaborative work in their classrooms. The teachers who want to try using the flipped classroom technique more often have Wade right in the building as a resource.

When the expert is a colleague, it can be hard not to invoke judgment ("Who does she think she is?") or self-judgment ("Who do I think I am?"). In any professional learning workshop—particularly in workshops given to a group of colleagues—the presenter can center the audience's learning instead of showcasing their own knowledge. A learner-centered workshop has the following three components:

- **Experiential:** Participants learn a specific practice they can use in their work by trying it themselves. There are different ways to lead an experiential exercise. Presenters can use a practice to teach about the practice itself. (Wade used the flipped classroom technique—watching a video and then doing collaborative work—to teach his colleagues about flipped learning.) Alternatively, the presenter can demonstrate the practice by having participants pretend they're students. For example, Wade could show one of his math videos to his colleagues and have them solve a challenging problem in groups.

  If participants do the same work that students do, they see what the work looks like in a classroom and can begin imagining it on their own. Some participants, however, might feel patronized if asked to pretend to be a student, or they might struggle to take that perspective. If some practices take too long to fit in the time allotted, the leader can create a smaller version for participants to experience.

Imagine, for example, that an English teacher has her students role-play a restorative justice circle as characters from *Lord of the Flies* (Golding, 1959/2016). She wants to show her colleagues how to use this practice but knows they haven't all read the book. Therefore, she has her colleagues role-play a restorative justice circle—but as characters from the children's book *Dragons Love Tacos* (Rubin & Salmieri, 2012), which she has time to read aloud at the beginning of the workshop.

- **Reflective:** Participants debrief the experience and examine how it can apply to their own practice. Although some participants might quickly see how they can use what they learned, others might need prompting. The presenter could try asking questions such as the following (filling in the blanks with the practice they've just demonstrated, such as flipping the classroom or role-playing a restorative justice circle):
    —What would you say are the main purposes of _____? Which of these purposes are most important to you?
    —If you were going to try _____, what unit would it be part of?
    —Which aspects of _____ seem most useful for your work?
    —How would you modify _____ to suit your subject, students, space, and timeframe?
    —Think of a few students who struggle in your class. How might _____ support their needs?
    —Think of a few students who excel in your class. How might _____ support their needs?

  Participants could answer questions like these in a whole-group discussion, or they could talk to partners, write privately in journals, have written conversations on large pieces of chart paper, or draw their responses. As insiders in the school community, both you and the presenter know your faculty culture well enough to decide which mode of reflection would be best.

- **Generative:** Participants make something to use in their own work, based on what they've just learned. Sometimes, teachers fail to implement a new practice they're excited about because they already have so much work to do. If teachers need to do or make something that will help them implement the practice they've just learned, the presenter can provide time for that work. For example, in the flipped classroom workshop, participants could start storyboarding their videos. In the restorative justice circle workshop, teachers could identify a harm that occurs in a book or historical event they teach about and start listing the characters or historical figures involved. They might not finish their storyboards or lists, let alone create an entire video or lesson plan, but if they *start,* they have unfinished work they might return to later. The presenter can check in with participants in the days or weeks following the workshop to ask how the work is going and provide support.

Figure 3.1 offers a planning tool for teachers to use when designing workshops for their colleagues.

As a leader, your role is to support workshop presenters so they're successful. You can meet with presenters to make sure they've planned experiential, reflective, and generative components that fit into the allotted timeframe. You can also relieve presenters of duties so they have more time to plan, help presenters gather necessary materials, and protect the time you've allocated for the workshop.

At the beginning of the workshop, introduce the presenter. Even though your faculty members already know this person as a colleague, they don't necessarily know what qualifies this person to present on a particular topic. For example, Wade's colleagues might know his name and recognize his face (although at a large school, even that might not be true), and they might think of him as an 11th grade math teacher, but they might not realize how much he knows about flipped classrooms. Just as you might introduce an outside expert by reading a short bio that includes their credentials, you can introduce an in-house expert by explaining what they do, how they learned to do it, and any effects you've noticed (whether on students, other constituents, or the school culture).

Finally, pay the presenter. Many districts and schools have a budget to hire outside experts or raise money from families and community partners. Why not use some of these funds to pay inside experts for their labor? Even a small honorarium acknowledges that this person has done work outside the scope of their job description and is being compensated for that work.

The Council

A teacher poses a question about how they can improve or expand in an area that matters to them. A group hears from this teacher, helps bring out new thinking, and shares their own experiences in this area.

Suggested group size: 4–6

Suggested time: 45–75 minutes

FIGURE 3.1

Workshop Planning Tool

Experiential

Participants learn how to use a tool or strategy by trying it out themselves.

Steps:

Materials:

Reflective

Participants debrief the experience and examine how it can apply to their work.

Questions:

Mode:

Generative

Participants create any materials they'll need to use what they've just learned.

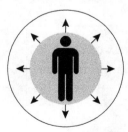

Instructions:

Examples:

Source: Copyright 2021 by Lauren Porosoff.

You can think of a council as the opposite of a workshop—the presenter seeks expertise instead of offering it. The presenter asks a question beginning with the words *How can I*: *How can I teach grammar more effectively? How can I teach U.S. geography using a creative project? How can I better prepare my students for the next test? How can I get Iain McArdle to talk in my class?*

For help with the identified issue, the presenter meets with a group of colleagues—a council of peers who will provide help. At the council meeting, the presenter describes exactly what's happening and what they want to see instead, and then they ask their *How can I* question. Group members make sure they fully understand the situation and the presenter's goals, and then the presenter listens silently while the group discusses the matter and offers insights.

Let's say a science teacher, Zora, notices that Iain never contributes to class discussions. If Zora asks the rest of Iain's teachers how they get him to talk, she might learn that he loves to discuss current events and then try connecting the science content to the news. Or Zora could bring her question to her department members to see how they encourage participation. She might discover that some teachers define *participation* more broadly and that while she's been focusing only on how often Iain speaks, she hasn't paid attention to how thoughtfully he listens or how thoroughly he takes notes. Zora might also learn new ways to elicit participation, such as through partner discussions and writing prompts. In any of these cases, presenting a question to her colleagues helps the teacher expand her understanding of the student, her own practices, or both.

By presenting a question, teachers benefit from the collective expertise of their colleagues, who in turn benefit from hearing and wrestling with a colleague's problem. Even if the groups don't *solve* the problem, presenters might leave feeling surprised by successes they hadn't noticed, inspired by their colleagues' insights, aware of new resources, and ready to try new methods. If nothing else, just hearing fellow educators recognize things we value and having them struggle along with us can be a tremendously powerful experience, and the whole group becomes stronger by working together toward the success of one of its members.

To structure the conversation, Figure 3.2 presents a council protocol: a step-by-step process for learning together that can be used repeatedly and across contexts. Though some people prefer to have a free-flowing discussion, learning histories and power dynamics affect the ways in which people contribute and listen. Protocols help everyone contribute something meaningful and ensure that all voices are equitably heard (McDonald, Mohr, Dichter, & McDonald, 2015; Porosoff, 2017).

FIGURE 3.2

Council Protocol

Assumptions

- Help-seeking is a sign of strength, not weakness.
- We can learn to give help with compassion and receive help with self-compassion.
- Reflecting on someone else's practice benefits our practice.

Preparation

1. One group member (the presenter) creates a *How can I* question about something that matters to them.
2. If necessary, the presenter gathers pieces of their own work, student work, quantitative data, or anything else that might demonstrate why they're asking the question.
3. The group chooses a facilitator, who makes sure the group sticks to the protocol, and a timekeeper, who ensures the group completes the protocol within the allotted time.

Process

1. *Hearing from the presenter.* The presenter explains what led them to ask their question. They describe particular experiences and, if helpful, show pieces of work. The presenter asks their *How can I* question and writes it down so the group can stay focused on it.
2. *Getting more information.* The group asks questions to get more information. These questions should have answers that are facts, not opinions or judgments:
   - Who...?
   - When...?
   - Where...?
   - What happened when...?
   - How many...?
3. *Bringing out new thinking.* The group asks questions to help the presenter think differently about the situation. Choose any questions that seem useful; don't try to get to them all. In addition to these example questions, the group can ask more of their own. The goal is to elicit new thinking, not self-judgment. Fill in any blanks with whatever comes after *How can I* in the presenter's question:
   - When did you first notice wanting to ___? How did it first become something you were concerned about?
   - Was there ever a time when you were able to ___, or do something similar? Describe the situation.
   - Have you read or heard anything about how to ___? Why weren't these resources helpful or satisfying?
   - Imagine the result of learning how to ___. What would be a smaller version of that? An even smaller version? What would be a bigger version? An even bigger version?
   - Imagine the result of learning how to ___. What would be the *opposite* situation? How would you achieve *that*?

   Group members take notes while the presenter speaks.

4. *Discussing the presenter's situation and the group's similar experiences.* The presenter listens and takes notes during the group discussion period. The goal is to talk about the presenter's situation and the group members' experiences, not to make suggestions. During this discussion, the group does not address the presenter directly so they can have a conversation about their own experiences. The following questions might help prompt discussion (fill in the blank as before, adapting the language, if necessary, to fit the group members' contexts):

— What seems important to the presenter?

— What did the presenter say that stood out to us?

— What did the presenter's situation make us think about or wonder?

— What have we read or heard about how to ___?

— In trying to ___, what *hasn't* worked for us?

— For those of us who have been able to ___, what does it look like, sound like, and feel like?

5. *Reflecting.* The group pauses so the presenter can reflect on what was just said.

6. *Sharing new thinking.* The presenter shares what they're thinking after hearing the group's discussion. The presenter might identify next steps they want to take, or they might simply share reactions to the ideas that came up.

7. Debriefing the experience.

— How did the presenter feel about this discussion?

— How did the group feel about this discussion?

— What did the group learn that might help them improve their teaching?

Source: Copyright 2021 by Lauren Porosoff.

Note that the group does not make suggestions during the protocol. Instead, members help the presenter clarify what's happening and think in new ways, and they share their similar experiences. The group's goal isn't so much to solve the presenter's problem—although that might happen—as it is to help the presenter think differently and notice possibilities.

For teachers to willingly seek help from their colleagues—and to make the discomfort associated with help-seeking worthwhile—they need to identify a meaningful learning or improving goal. Ask your faculty to think about what they want to know more about, understand more fully, be able to do, or get better at. You might offer some sentence starters such as these:

- I want to know more about ___.
- I want to understand ___ more fully.
- I want to be able to ___.
- I want to get better at ___.
- I want to learn more ways to ___.

- I want to learn more reliable ways to ___.
- I wish I could ___.
- I'm frustrated that I can't seem to ___.
- I worry that I don't ___.

Those last two sentence starters might sound negative, so if you use them, emphasize that the point is to notice feelings of frustration and worry (which can indicate that something important is at stake), not to dwell on failure. Whichever prompts you provide, make sure the teachers know they'll share their responses with you only if they choose to.

Next, ask teachers to mark one learning or improving goal that feels particularly important to them and turn that goal into a question that begins with the words *How can I*. Here are some examples of such questions:

- How can I teach grammar more effectively?
- How can I develop a project for the Cold War unit?
- How can I make sure my students are better prepared for their chemistry tests in the future?
- How can I get Iain McArdle to talk in my class?
- How can I bring more diverse literature into my curriculum?
- How can I encourage students to read more diverse books on their own?
- How can I encourage students to challenge themselves?
- How can I make my classroom safer and more inclusive for transgender students?
- How can I embed social-emotional learning into my academic class?
- How can I fight burnout?

In addition to these, try sharing your own genuine *How can I* questions, whether they're about teaching or leadership. If you make yourself vulnerable first, the teachers with whom you work will know you're not asking them to do anything you're not willing to do yourself.

The mere act of writing questions about their practices might make some teachers feel uncomfortable. They might wonder how their questions will make them look to their colleagues or whether anyone will have a useful response. Some might just think, *I hate stuff like this.*

Although you can't take away thoughts and feelings like these, you can acknowledge them. Try asking teachers how they feel about themselves as a result of turning their meaningful learning goals into questions they might ask their colleagues. They might not enjoy asking for help or even writing the questions, but they might feel some satisfaction knowing that they're working toward goals that matter to them.

Once teachers have written their *How can I* questions, their next step is submitting their questions to you so you can create council groups. Ideally, some teachers will volunteer to be presenters. You can hand out index cards and invite teachers to write their names, their questions, and a rating of how willing they are to present their questions to a group of colleagues. Once you have that information, you can strategically choose presenters who have some power in the community, or you can choose those who are most willing to present.

The Exemplar Study

> *Teachers analyze multiple diverse examples of excellent work their colleagues created so they can learn more ways to create the same type of work themselves.*
>
> *Suggested group size: 10–12*
>
> *Suggested time: 30–45 minutes*

When teachers give an assignment, they often show their students *exemplars:* examples of excellent work of the type they are about to create. Before students write their own sonnets, they read sonnets. Before they make their own public service announcements, they watch public service announcements. Seeing multiple exemplars helps students notice requirements and possibilities. If all the exemplars have a particular feature in common (such as how all sonnets have 14 lines), then students' work should also have that feature. If the exemplars vary in a particular way (such as how sonnets can be about any topic), then students can choose what they do. Perhaps most important, if students see how work reflects its creator's values, then they, too, can create work that reflects their values.

Just as looking at exemplars helps students understand their task and make choices, teachers can look at exemplars for guidance when they create their work—lesson plans, assignments, rubrics, tests, classroom displays, learning stations, furniture arrangements, curriculum maps, comments on student work, websites, emails to families, and social media posts. In an exemplar study (adapted from a student protocol of the same name in Porosoff & Weinstein, 2020), teachers learn from their colleagues' excellent work—so they can imagine new possibilities for themselves.

During the protocol, the group looks at several examples of the same type of work. The Exploring Exemplars chart (Figure 3.3) helps teachers keep track of their observations. You can use this chart or make your own, substituting the word *work* with *assignment, unit plan, classroom display,* or whatever the teachers are looking at. The questions in the chart are designed to help teachers notice that their work products can reflect their values. In articulating what matters to the colleagues who created the exemplars, participants set themselves up to consider how their work can reflect what matters to them.

Sometimes when teachers look at multiple exemplars, they start to compare and evaluate them, making statements such as, "This one's my favorite" or "I like the formatting of this one, but the language on that one is much clearer." Although it's normal for them to have preferences, encourage participants to focus on what makes them curious as opposed to what they like—and how their colleagues' values might have guided decisions. For example, a teacher might prefer a rubric that describes multiple levels of performance, but why might someone only describe effective performance? What does that colleague want students to think about or do? How would including only descriptions of effective performance achieve that goal? Participants don't need to decide which rubric is better or even which goal is better; the point is for them to connect their colleagues' choices to goals and those goals to values, so that they, too, can make values-conscious choices in creating their work.

To prepare for this exercise, you'll need to collect at least four (and preferably more) pieces of teacher work of the same type. Including more than four exemplars means that teachers can choose which ones they analyze. The more diverse the exemplars, the more options teachers will become aware of. For example, if participants are looking at rubrics that all have point values for each criterion, teachers will assume that their rubrics should have point values for each criterion—and maybe that's the goal. However, if some rubrics use verbal descriptors such as *excellent, effective,* and *basic,* then teachers will know they have this option.

Figure 3.4 presents the protocol to use for the exemplar study.

Depending on the group, you might include work by teachers of the same subject or grade level, or you might intentionally show examples of the same type of work from different subjects and grade levels. For example, if 6th grade math teachers were to use this protocol to look at rubrics, they might look only at 6th grade math

FIGURE 3.3				
Exploring Exemplars Chart				
	Work #1:	Work #2:	Work #3:	Work #4:
What seems important to the teacher who created this?				
What does this teacher want their students to think about or do?				
What's something this teacher chose to do that makes you curious?				
What's interesting or effective about that choice?				
What, if anything, confuses you or gives you pause?				

Source: From *Two-for-One Teaching: Connecting Instruction to Student Values* (p. 148), by L. Porosoff and J. Weinstein, 2020. Bloomington, IN: Solution Tree. Copyright 2020 Solution Tree. Adapted with permission.

FIGURE 3.4

Exemplar Study Protocol

Assumptions

- All the work we're about to see is good work.
- No work is perfect.
- The colleagues who created these pieces of work are sharing them so that others can learn.
- The group will say what makes them curious and what they want to try in their own work, not praise or criticize the work they see today.

Preparation

1. The group leader, or a group member acting as the leader for purposes of this protocol, collects several exemplars of the same type of work. These can be lesson plans, assignments, rubrics, tests, classroom displays, learning stations, furniture arrangements, curriculum maps, comments on student work, websites, e-mails to families, social media posts, or any other type of work.

2. The group chooses a facilitator, who makes sure the group sticks to the protocol and leads the discussion and share-out at the end (steps 4–6), and a timekeeper, who ensures the group completes the protocol within the allotted time.

3. Group members receive copies of the Exploring Exemplars chart (Figure 3.3).

Process

1. *Surveying the exemplars.* Participants look at several excellent pieces of work of the same type. If there are more than four exemplars, the participants take some time to look at them all and select four to analyze.

2. *Analyzing the exemplars.* Participants fill out their Exploring Exemplars charts (Figure 3.3), individually and silently so as to avoid biasing one another's observations.

3. *Listing features of this type of work.* The facilitator leads the group in listing features all the exemplars share and then discussing whether all work of this type should have these features.

4. *Learning from the exemplars.* The facilitator leads the group in a discussion about what they can learn from their colleagues' choices, using the following questions:
   - What did your colleagues do in their work that you want to try in yours?
   - What did you see that you're curious about but aren't yet willing or ready to try? What would help you become more willing or ready to try it?
   - What are some of the values you share with the colleagues who created the work you looked at today?

5. *Writing commitment statements.* Each participant writes the words *I will,* writes a next step for their own work, writes the word *because,* and finishes the sentence with why they're taking this step.

6. *Sharing (optional).* Participants can choose to share their commitment statements with the group or keep their commitments private.

Source: From *Two-for-One Teaching: Connecting Instruction to Student Values* (pp. 149–150), by L. Porosoff and J. Weinstein, 2020. Bloomington, IN: Solution Tree. Copyright 2020 Solution Tree. Adapted with permission.

rubrics, or they might look at rubrics used by their colleagues who teach 7th or 8th grade math or by teachers of other subjects. Looking at a more diverse set of exemplars helps teachers focus more on the work's form and function, as opposed to its specific content.

Depending on the type of work you use, you might have to take certain steps to make the exemplars available for analysis. For example, you might have to print out rubrics or curriculum maps, take pictures of classroom displays or furniture arrangements, or send an email with links to websites or social media accounts. Instead of making enough copies of each exemplar so everyone has their own, consider putting out just one of each and having teachers walk around the room to look at the different pieces of work together. Either way, be sure to number the exemplars so the group can easily refer to each one.

Finally, remove the names of the teachers who created the exemplars, along with any student names, if you can. Other details might enable participants to guess whose work is whose, though. On a grade-level team that has only one science teacher, if you show a science assignment, everyone knows who wrote it. The exemplar study will feel different when the work is anonymous than when it isn't. In any case, it's helpful to remind participants that their goal is to learn from the work, not to evaluate it.

The Toolbox Share

> *Each person describes their own practices in a particular area. After everyone has shared, each group member identifies a next step so they can continue to grow in this area.*
>
> *Suggested group size: 6–8*
>
> *Suggested time: 45–60 minutes*

So far, the learning formats we've seen position some teachers as experts and others as learners. This format, the toolbox share, positions everyone as an expert who has something meaningful to contribute to everyone else's practice. Rather than hearing about a "best" practice and narrowing the group's repertoire to include only that practice, members expand and diversify their repertoires to include any and all practices that help students learn.

The toolbox share begins with a *How do we* question. For example, *How do we integrate artistic expression into academic classes? How do we break the news to parents and guardians when a student misbehaves? How do we examine our resources for bias? How do we respond when we uncover bias?*

These are not *How should we* questions, which ask about "right" ways of doing something or "best" practices. Nor are they *How would we* questions, which posit a different set of circumstances, or *How could we* questions, which explore alternative possibilities. Rather, *How do we* questions invite teachers to share what they're currently doing in their existing situations.

Figure 3.5 presents the protocol to use for the toolbox share. It includes two go-arounds, which means everyone in the room has exactly two chances to speak. After hearing the *How do we* question and taking a few moments to think about it, everyone takes a turn to respond. While any one person speaks, everyone else writes down that person's name and some part of what the person says. After more reflection, everyone shares a next step they'll take as a result of what they've just heard. To ensure that everyone has an equal voice and gets an equal amount of attention, the protocol intentionally does not include opportunities for colleagues to ask one another questions or to dialogue. If group members want to hear more from one another, they can follow up later. Think of the toolbox share as a beginning of *many* conversations rather than as *the* conversation.

FIGURE 3.5

Toolbox Share Protocol

Assumptions
- Everyone, including novices, has something meaningful to contribute.
- Everyone, including very experienced practitioners, benefits from reflecting on their practices and considering new possibilities.
- Groups benefit from coming together and listening to each member.

Preparation
1. The group leader (or a group member who is acting as a leader for purposes of this learning event) identifies a *How do we* question about the group's area of practice.
2. The group chooses a facilitator, who makes sure the group sticks to the protocol, and a timekeeper, who ensures the group completes the protocol within the allotted time.

Process
1. *Introducing the question and order.* A group member states the *How do we* question. Someone in the group volunteers to respond first. An order is established so that everyone has a turn and knows when it is.

2. *Collecting thoughts.* Group members take a few minutes to write what they want to say in response to the question. This allows each person to share their most important ideas succinctly.

3. *Responding and tracking.* Each member of the group takes a turn responding while everyone else writes down the person's name and a small part of what they said. By the time everyone has shared, each member of the group has a list that includes each other person's name and something they said.

4. *Reflecting.* After everyone has shared, each person silently reads over their notes, using the following prompts to help them reflect on what they heard:
   — Which idea sounds most *appealing* to you right now? Mark it with an *A*.
   — Which sounds most *useful* for your practice? Mark it with a *U*.
   — Which sounds most *different* from what your practice usually looks like? Mark it with a *D*.

5. *Sharing next steps.* Each group member takes a turn sharing something they'll try or a next step they'll take. The group leader records these statements. Next steps might involve trying someone's practice or a version of it; connecting with a group member to ask questions, observe them teaching, visit their classroom, or borrow a resource; gathering data; reflecting alone or with others; or continuing to learn in some other way.

Source: Copyright 2021 by Lauren Porosoff.

Figure 3.6 presents a note-taking organizer for group members to use during Step 3 of the toolbox share. Because the format—writing down someone's name and a small part of what they say—might be unfamiliar and therefore difficult to visualize, the note-taking organizer offers a guide. It has seven spaces for writing notes, because ideal groups will have no more than eight people, and participants take notes about one another but not themselves.

As the leader, your job is to pose a *How do we* question or solicit one from your team, department, or faculty. The question can be about any meaningful aspect of teaching, such as curriculum, instructional design, pedagogy, assessment, resource use, time management, or communication. It might be about an existing school priority. For example, at a school that has been working to incorporate the United Nations' Sustainable Development Goals into the curriculum, each academic department might meet for a toolbox share using the question *How do we use the United Nations' Sustainable Development Goals in our courses?* Alternatively, a single department or team could ask a question that applies only to them. For example, a 9th grade team might ask the question *How do we help our students transition from middle school to high school?*

You might transform parent or student concerns into *How do we* questions for teachers. Maybe, for example, you've heard parents complain that their kids have too much homework. You could pose the question *How do we limit our students' workload?* or *How do we ensure students have time for their families, personal interests, and self-care*

FIGURE 3.6

Toolbox Share Note-Taking Organizer

Source: Copyright 2021 by Lauren Porosoff.

after school? Using a concern from a constituent group for a toolbox share puts the matter on teachers' radar, gives everyone new ways to address it, and makes teachers aware of helpful practices they're already using (and perhaps could use more frequently).

If you participate in the toolbox share, you can quickly assess whether your faculty simply needs to make better use of practices they already know or whether they need a new set of strategies (or a new way of thinking about the topic).

Finally, you can simply ask teachers to share their *How do we* questions. What do they want to know about their colleagues' practices? Here are some examples of questions you can share with teachers to prompt them to think of their own:

- How do we assess students fairly?
- How do we make room for students to be creative?
- How do we lead conversations about race?
- How do we incorporate service learning into our programs?
- How do we gamify learning?
- How do we use our classroom spaces to promote learning?
- How do we ensure 100 percent participation?
- How do we teach students how to show compassion to one another?
- How do we give our students brain and body breaks?
- How do we support students who are grieving?

If you ask teachers to come up with questions, you can send a simple survey in advance of the toolbox share and then choose a question to bring to the group. Alternatively, you can arrange a preliminary meeting for teachers to generate *How do we* questions. They can either pass their questions to you (on index cards, for example) or they can take turns sharing their questions and choose one together.

Having teachers generate, share, and discuss their questions—and then choose one for the protocol—takes time, but that work can be rewarding. Once, I was teaching the toolbox share protocol to educators from various New York City independent schools, and I had them form groups based on their roles: classroom teachers, principals, assistant principals, department heads, and so on. One group was composed of diversity, equity, and inclusion (DEI) practitioners—people who had titles such as *director of community life* or *diversity coordinator*. Excited to lead everyone through the toolbox share protocol so they could then go back and use it at their schools, I asked the groups to quickly generate *How do we* questions, share them, and then choose one to use for the protocol.

This was just a training exercise, meant more to teach them how to use the protocol itself than to focus on any particular content. But I discovered that all the groups wanted a lot more time to share and discuss their questions than I had anticipated. The DEI group took the longest. As departments of one at their schools, and often as one of the few BIPOC faculty members at predominantly white institutions, they so rarely had opportunities to share their practices and learn from others in their area of expertise. Don't underestimate how important it will be for teachers to share their questions and decide by consensus on one to explore—especially if they're asking about practices that matter to them and that they haven't had enough opportunities to talk about.

At the same time, if you ask a group to agree on a question, then members with the loudest voices or the most power might be the ones who actually decide. Some members might feel uncomfortable arguing why the group should discuss a different question or even reading their genuine *How do we* questions out loud.

In a department, team, or faculty that has unspoken power and privilege dynamics (and many do), you can solicit questions ahead of time and choose one yourself. In that case, consider asking teachers to explain why their *How do we* questions are important both to them as practitioners and for student learning. Whether you gather questions in advance or on the spot, asking teachers to share their questions will give you a window into what matters to the people you lead.

The Intervision Group

> *Colleagues visit one another's classrooms and offer nonjudgmental feedback: observations, questions, interpretations, and inspirations. Each teacher then reflects on how they'll use the feedback they received.*
>
> *Suggested group size: 3*
>
> *Suggested time: 20 minutes for each classroom visit, 10 minutes for each postvisit discussion, and 45 minutes for the final meeting*

As part of your leadership role, you might visit teachers' classrooms to observe them. That's *supervision:* someone with more institutional power observes someone with less to evaluate that person's performance. Because some teachers associate classroom observations with supervision, they might feel a little nervous about hosting an observer. But there are other reasons for classroom observations besides supervision. In *intervision,* peers observe one another so everyone can grow.

Similarly, many teachers associate feedback with judgment. Those judgments might be positive ("That was a great response to Alejandra's comment") or negative ("Matan's group seemed a little off task"). We sometimes try to hide negative judgment under a question ("How do you think Matan's group did?") or a suggestion ("Next time, you might try giving one direction at a time so students don't get overwhelmed"). However we deliver the feedback, if we imply that something could have been better, it's criticism.

Any kind of judgment positions the giver of that feedback as the authority. The receiver can agree or disagree with the judgment, but either way, they're in the passive position of being judged. The intervision group protocol keeps everyone on equal footing by having colleagues share their experiences in one another's classrooms—their observations, questions, interpretations, and inspirations—rather than praise, criticism, suggestions, or any other kind of judgment.

Based on their colleagues' experiences, each teacher can make decisions about whether their classroom creates the kind of experience they want—or whether they want to make changes. When they visit their colleagues, they also learn from what they see. Thus, each teacher learns from visiting colleagues and from being visited by colleagues. Figure 3.7 presents a protocol to use for intervision groups. Each member of the group takes a turn as the "subject" whose class is observed, the "noticer" who points out things that draw their attention, and the "questioner" who asks about things that make them curious. After each has been in all three roles, the group meets to discuss all three classroom visits and share their learning.

FIGURE 3.7

Intervision Group Protocol

Assumptions
- Highly experienced and skilled teachers can learn from observing their colleagues, and less experienced and skilled teachers do things their colleagues would benefit from observing.
- Any teacher can learn something important from hearing a colleague's observations, questions, interpretations, and inspirations.
- All teachers in the group are equals. This is not supervision and will not include judgmental remarks of any kind, including praise, criticism, or suggestions.

---

continued

FIGURE 3.7 (*continued*)

Intervision Group Protocol

Preparation

- The group determines times when each person in the group can be observed by the other two, and a time when all three group members can meet together.
- Each group member may wish to share a bit about the lesson their colleagues will see.

Process

1. *Assigning roles.* There will be three rounds of intervision, one for each teacher in the group. For the first round, assign roles: the "subject" (whose class will be observed during this round), the "noticer" (who will write down things they see and hear), and the "questioner" (who will write questions they have about anything that makes them curious).
2. *Visiting the class.* The noticer and the questioner visit the subject's class and stay for at least 20 minutes. While there, the noticer writes observations—anything they see or hear that stands out for any reason. Meanwhile, the questioner writes down questions about anything that makes them curious. The observations and questions can be about anything the teacher does, anything the students do, or anything else in the room.
3. *Writing interpretations.* The noticer and questioner work together to write their interpretations of what seems important to the subject.
4. *Writing inspirations.* The noticer and questioner, individually and without discussion, write down at least one inspiration: something important that the visit made them want to try in their own practice or keep thinking about.
5. *Repeating the process for all teachers.* Steps 1–4 repeat two more times, so that everyone gets a chance to be the subject, the noticer, and the questioner.
6. *Sharing feedback.* After all three classroom visits have occurred, the group comes together to review the notes from each visit. While hearing their colleagues share, each teacher can choose to respond to any observations, questions, interpretations, or inspirations—and can also choose to just listen.
7. *Reflecting on learning.* Group members reflect on their learning, privately in writing or together in a conversation, using the following questions:
   - As a result of visiting your two colleagues' classes, what might you do differently in yours?
   - Are your colleague's observations the things you'd hope would stand out? If not, what might you change?
   - Do your colleague's questions indicate a need to make anything clearer or more specific for your students? If so, how will you do that?
   - Do your colleagues' interpretations of what matters to you match up with what you think is important? If not, what can you change so that your classroom space, lessons, assignments, and interactions better reflect your values?
   - Are your colleagues' inspirations the things you'd hope someone would take away from visiting you? What else would you hope someone would learn from watching you?
8. *Debriefing the process.* The group has a short discussion about the intervision process, using these two questions:
   - How did it feel to *offer* our observations, questions, interpretations, and inspirations to one another?
   - How did it feel to *hear* our group members' observations, questions, interpretations, and inspirations?

Source: From *Two-for-One Teaching: Connecting Instruction to Student Values* (pp. 169–175), by L. Porosoff and J. Weinstein, 2020. Bloomington, IN: Solution Tree. Copyright 2020 Solution Tree. Adapted with permission.

Figure 3.8 presents a note-taking organizer to use during intervision. It has spaces for the noticer and questioner to write the subject's name (as well as their own) and to take notes. The *Observations, Questions,* and *Inspiration* spaces are on one or the other side of the chart, indicating that each person will write notes individually, whereas the *Interpretations* space spans both sides, indicating that both the noticer and the questioner will write these notes together. It might be a little awkward for two people to write on the same sheet, but it allows the teacher who was observed to receive one set of notes.

If you announce that everyone will participate in intervision (or even that everyone will be invited to participate), expect some anxiety, because many teachers equate classroom visits with performance evaluation and feedback with judgment. You can use this opportunity to distinguish supervision from intervision, and judgmental feedback—praise, criticism, and suggestions—from the nonjudgmental feedback they'll give one another.

Some teachers might ask what's wrong with praise. Praise makes people feel good, and teachers don't get enough appreciation. You can explain that colleagues are always welcome to praise and appreciate one another. However, this PD activity leaves all forms of judgment out—so everyone stays on equal footing and so all teachers can decide for themselves whether and how they want to change, based on hearing someone else's experience of their work.

The Bringback

> *A faculty member brings back a resource to share with colleagues, who then discuss how it applies to their work.*
>
> *Suggested group size: 3–5*
>
> *Suggested time: 45–75 minutes, depending on the group size and resource complexity*

The bringback might be the most empowering professional learning structure because *no one* is an expert. Everyone learns together. Imagine that at a conference, Ines attends a session on how to gamify instruction to enhance student learning. She downloads the slide deck from the conference website and brings it to her next 7th

FIGURE 3.8

Intervision Note-Taking Organizer

Subject:

Noticer:

Questioner:

Interpretations:

Inspiration:

Inspiration:

grade team meeting. Her colleagues look at the slides and then discuss how they might use gamification in their classes. The science teacher thinks her students could play a game to learn how DNA transcription works. The history teacher says he loves playing the game Codenames and can imagine making his own sets of cards to help his students learn key terms for each unit. The Spanish teacher says she once tried having her class play the Spanish-language versions of popular children's games but thought it took too long to explain; now she's talking about reviving that activity using the guidelines Ines brought back from her conference.

Importantly, Ines is not holding herself out as an expert on gamified learning just because she went to one session on it. She also is not attempting to convince her colleagues that gamified learning is the greatest thing to happen to pedagogy since Paulo Freire. She's not even promising that *she'll* use gamification. Rather, she's just sharing something cool she learned so her colleagues can learn about it, too. In a bringback, teachers explore and experiment together—just as we hope they have their students do.

Figure 3.9 presents a protocol to use for bringbacks. It has three rounds of discussion: exploratory (Steps 3–4), pragmatic (Steps 5–6), and critical (Steps 7–8). When we read or hear about a new idea, we often jump immediately to judgment: Do we like this or not? If we like something, we might adopt it without fully interrogating its limits. If we *don't* like something, we might dismiss it without considering which parts might be usable or even understanding what it is. The bringback protocol slows participants down so they fully explore the resource and imagine its applications before judging it.

Though you can use the bringback format to share articles, videos, and other resources you encounter, it's also an opportunity to ask teachers to share work *they* encounter. You could probably create many years' worth of meaningful PD just by regularly sending out calls for resources to your faculty and then building bringbacks around those resources.

You also might take a broad view of which resources could be useful for teachers to explore together. Sometimes, teachers benefit from looking at resources designed specifically for their area of practice. For example, a science department could read *Science in the City: Culturally Relevant STEM Education* (Brown, 2019), or a 2nd grade team could watch the TED Talk "Creative Ways to Get Kids to Thrive in School" (Della Flora, 2019). Other times, teachers could study a resource that applies to all subjects and grade levels.

FIGURE 3.9

Bringback Protocol

Assumptions

- Even the strongest teachers can benefit from incorporating new resources.
- We cannot know the full potential of new material unless and until we have a conversation about it.
- Even if the material turns out not to be useful to all of us, the conversation still is. Having conversations with colleagues is inherently valuable.

Preparation

1. A member of the group (the "bringer") identifies a resource such as an article, handouts from a conference, or a video for the group to study together.
2. The group chooses a facilitator, who makes sure the group sticks to the protocol, a timekeeper, who ensures the group completes the protocol within the allotted time, and a scribe, who takes notes.
3. If the group is reading or viewing a longer work, copies are distributed in advance.

Process

1. *Introducing the material.* The bringer briefly introduces the material by explaining how they discovered it and summarizing what it's about. At this time, the bringer does not explain or interpret the resource, offer any suggestions about how or why it might be used, or answer questions about its content.
2. *Reading or viewing.* Everyone in the group reads or views the material. If the group is discussing a longer work they've already read or viewed, they take a few moments to review their notes silently.
3. *Asking exploratory ("What is this?") questions.* Each member of the group takes a turn to respond to any (but not necessarily all) of the following questions:
   - What makes me curious?
   - What components, features, or frameworks stand out?
   - What's familiar about this?
   - What's new or different about this?
   - Which aspects connect to the mission of our group, organization, or professional community?
4. *Summarizing exploratory responses.* The group notices and names important connections and outliers among the responses. The scribe takes notes.
5. *Asking pragmatic ("How could we apply this?") questions.* Each member of the group takes a turn to respond to any (but not necessarily all) of the following questions:
   - What would this look like in my practice?
   - Which parts seem most applicable?
   - What problems does this illuminate or solve?
   - When would I invoke or implement this?
   - How would this enhance my work?

6. *Summarizing pragmatic responses.* The group notices and names important connections and outliers among the responses. The scribe takes notes.

7. *Asking critical ("What are the limits of this?") questions.* Each member of the group takes a turn to respond to any (but not necessarily all) of the following questions:
   — Which parts seem incomplete or irrelevant?
   — What problems could this cause or exacerbate?
   — What biases does this reflect?
   — What might be some of the costs in terms of time, space, energy, money, or status?
   — Do the benefits seem worth the costs?

8. *Summarizing critical responses.* The group notices and names important connections and outliers among the responses. The scribe takes notes.

9. *Deciding on next steps.* The group identifies actions for each member and a timeline for those actions. If there is disagreement on what to do next, the group might agree to do another reading, have further discussions, or attend an outside professional learning event together. Some members of the group may wish to pilot a program or create a prototype, study the results, and bring their data back to the group.

10. *Debriefing the experience.*
    — What did we learn from this discussion?
    — What was useful about the discussion itself or anything raised in it?
    — What are we still curious about?

Source: Copyright 2021 by Lauren Porosoff.

Alternatively, teachers could use a resource that explicitly applies to another subject or grade level but conceptually applies to theirs. For example, in the article "How Should We Sing Happy Birthday?" (Elson, 2019), a white K–1 teacher interrogates what she'd considered *the* birthday song and describes a unit on culturally relevant birthday celebrations. Even though middle school teachers probably wouldn't celebrate birthdays the same way as teachers in an early elementary class—nor would they use Elson's birthday song unit—her article could launch an important discussion of how educators bring their backgrounds and assumptions to all kinds of classroom celebrations, as well as how to make celebrations more inclusive and meaningful for all students.

Finally, consider using resources from outside the teaching field for bringbacks. Ideas from other helping professions (such as psychology, social work, and nursing), design disciplines (such as architecture, urban planning, and visual communication), politics, or business might apply to teaching and learning. Imagine that a group of educators discusses "Engineering Social Incentives for Health" (Asch & Rosin, 2016), an article about how social relationships can get people to choose healthier behaviors. Even though the article is written for medical professionals, teachers who read it might think of new ideas for how social relationships could incentivize academic behaviors in their classrooms.

Every field has its own concepts, vocabulary, assumptions, and research base. If a resource has an intended audience outside teaching, teachers *must* break free from their usual ways of seeing their work and think creatively about how to apply these new ideas to their practice. That kind of creative thinking is potentially interesting for the teachers involved and might lead to innovations for their classrooms—or even for the teaching field!

Just as an exercise, visit the website of a magazine written for helping, design, political, or business professionals. Click on any article; as you read it, ask yourself how you could apply its ideas to your work at school.

Building a Culture of Risk Taking

Although inviting an outsider to deliver professional development might be expensive and ultimately unhelpful, it's *safe*. No one in the community has to put their own practices out in front of the colleagues they see every day.

In-house professional learning carries more risk. Certainly, those who expose frustrations and mistakes to a council, or who invite an intervision group into their classrooms where anything could happen, risk embarrassing themselves or feeling inadequate. But sharing expertise in a workshop, or work products for an exemplar study, can feel even riskier. Those who display their knowledge might draw envy or criticism. Workshop presenters might stumble over their words, not know the answer to a colleague's question, or bore the audience. Even in toolbox share and bringback sessions, where everyone is positioned as equals, colleagues with conflicting ideas might bicker—or worse, they might politely disagree but then gossip about each other. In any group, members might monopolize the conversation, stay silent for fear of seeming ignorant or incompetent, exclude or gang up on one person, interrupt or dismiss one another's contributions, roll their eyes, sigh, check their phones, make insensitive or offensive remarks, or otherwise derail the learning experience.

The structures in this chapter are designed to reduce some of these disruptive behaviors—by allowing only certain types of comments, creating equitable systems of turn taking, including private reflection and optional sharing, and limiting group sizes.

However, the structures themselves only go so far, especially if some people either don't take the time to understand the guidelines or deliberately disregard them.

Some schools use get-to-know-you activities, discussion norms, or safe-space declarations in attempts to create environments in which people can be vulnerable. Such practices can help set a tone, but they don't necessarily work. Simply declaring that this is a safe space does not make it so, establishing norms doesn't mean people will follow them, and doing activities that help people get to know one another doesn't mean they'll be vulnerable afterward.

But as a leader, you can build a culture of risk taking in three important ways:

- *Don't just organize participatory professional learning events; participate in them yourself.* If you invite teachers to present their questions to councils of their peers, present a question of your own. If your faculty is working in intervision groups, make your own group with two other leaders. If you ask teachers to have a bringback discussion, join in, especially if you know very little about its topic. When your faculty sees you participating, they'll know you're willing to do the work you're asking them to do, that you'll make yourself vulnerable for the sake of professional growth, and that your school is a place where they can take risks.

  Participating in the PD will also help you relate better to teachers who feel hesitant or disappointed. You'll be able to say things like, "I'm nervous about my workshop, too" or "I felt distracted because I was trying to finish the article, so next time we do a bringback, I'm going to listen more carefully, even if it means I don't read everything." After making statements such as these, you can explain why the work is worthwhile anyway—not just for the school but for you personally—and thus model taking risks in the service of your values so they can take risks in the service of theirs.

- *Ask people with high status, access, and visibility—such as a department chair or member of the "old guard"—to go first in situations that require the most risk,* or go first yourself as a leader. When this happens, those with less power know that no one is above challenging themselves, trying something new, learning more, or asking for help.

  What constitutes a *risk* will depend on an individual's history and relationships, the school's culture, and other factors. Imagine a middle school principal is preparing her faculty to use the council format. She informs the group that her *How can I* question is *How can I communicate more effectively with families?* If this principal already communicates well with families, or if family engagement has never been one of her priorities, then teachers might think she's choosing an easy issue and therefore choose easy issues themselves. Worse, they might perceive her as disingenuous for telling them to share their authentic struggles while she's not sharing hers.

However, if this principal got in trouble for mishandling communication about a controversial speaker, if teachers regularly complain about her long-winded and confusing emails, or if she's previously said she lacks confidence in her own writing skills, then her faculty will understand that asking about effective communication is an act of vulnerability. If she shares her own discomfort in asking the question and explains why she's asking anyway, then she's letting teachers know that they, too, might find it rewarding to open up.

- *Check in with the most vulnerable teachers at your school.* These might be teachers who are new to the profession or to your geographic area, belong to a historically marginalized group, or teach subjects that get deprioritized at your school. Consider whether there are individual teachers or groups of teachers at your school who aren't taken as seriously as they should be or who are unseen, unheard, disrespected, or misrepresented on your faculty. Although you may hear "We care about everyone" or "That would never happen here," watch out for effects of bias anyway. Sending a quick email to ask how someone felt in a session or stopping by someone's classroom to see how they're doing demonstrates your commitment to keeping everyone safe.

Sharing Responsibility for Success

As a child, my favorite museum was the American Museum of Natural History in New York. Every time we went, we'd gape at the apatosaurus, stand under the blue whale and hope it didn't fall on our heads, and touch the crystals that seemed to glow from within. If you visited a natural history museum in the '80s or '90s, you might have similar memories, because when the only way to interact with an exhibit is as a spectator, designers "focus on making the content consistent and high quality, so that every visitor, regardless of her background or interests, receives a reliably good experience" (Simon, 2010, p. 2).

PD is similar. A keynote speaker's only job is to give a high-quality presentation, and if we attend, our only job is to listen. Although we might not be equally excited or moved, we all hear the same words and see the same slides. We all receive the same message, even if we interpret it differently. But when people participate, they co-construct their experiences, which will therefore be different.

In *The Participatory Museum,* Nina Simon (2010) describes a cleverly designed exhibit for a historic blast furnace. Visitors received special flashlights they could shine on different parts of the blast furnace to activate explanations, stories, and sensory events. We can imagine at least three ways visitors might interact with this exhibit. Some might carefully scan the entire blast furnace, and they might leave feeling satisfied that they saw everything or annoyed that they had to be so methodical. Others might shine their flashlights only on areas of interest; they might leave feeling glad they could attend to parts that made them curious without wasting time on parts that didn't—or they might feel disappointed that only some parts interested them. Still others might randomly flash their lights around, triggering content at random. These visitors might leave having enjoyed their own spontaneous approach and the exhibit's little surprises, or they might feel like they missed something important and didn't take the exhibit seriously enough. Each of these visitors would have a different experience based on what matters to them (thoroughness, curiosity, or playfulness), but all would be partially responsible for the quality of their experience, because they actively chose it.

When we make PD participatory, we can't guarantee that everyone has the same experience—which means we can't guarantee the quality of any *one* person's experience. Instead, we must recognize that different people will have different experiences based on their choices and that how satisfied they feel afterward depends in part on them.

I know what it's like to have a bad experience of good PD because of my own choices. The Bard Institute of Writing and Thinking teaches educators how to use writing to help students discover and deepen their thinking. I've taken several of their courses and love the creative prompts and the ideas we generate through our writing and conversations. Once, though, we got a prompt I just didn't like. Although I don't remember the prompt itself, I remember feeling annoyed that I had nothing to say in response. Instead of wrestling with the prompt or searching for a way to *make* it relevant, I petulantly refused to write. When it was time to share, everyone else had something to say, but I had to pass. At that point, I was even more annoyed because I knew I was responsible for my own disappointment. I'd missed an opportunity not because it was a bad prompt but because I was unwilling to create a meaningful experience out of it.

In any participatory experience, giving away some of the power means also giving away some of the responsibility to make choices that lead to a meaningful and satisfying outcome. As the curator, you have the responsibility to create events in which teachers can potentially learn something important, but whether they *choose* to learn is up to them.

Onward

In this chapter, we explored six different ways to structure peer-to-peer professional learning so everyone can participate. In Chapter 4, we'll look at how to integrate these structures into a purposeful and cohesive professional learning unit.

Make It Cohesive: Organizing Professional Learning

In *Inside the Lost Museum,* professor of American studies Steven Lubar (2017) explains that creating a sense of cohesiveness is at the core of a curator's work: "System, arrangement, and juxtaposition—whether a chronological beginning, middle, and end, a taxonomic sequence, contrasts and comparisons, or a narrative—are the foundations of exhibitions. Choosing a story to tell, and then choosing and arranging the objects to tell it: at the most basic level, that's the art of exhibition" (p. 178). As viewers, we might choose to take in the entire story, scoot past the boring parts so we can get to the exciting ones, backtrack to details we missed, or ignore the structure by skipping around. But we know a story *exists*.

Just as an exhibition curator's work is to create a meaningful context for people to understand and interact with art, a PD curator creates a meaningful context for teachers to understand and interact with new ideas and practices. Curators, whether of art or PD, design a coherent set of experiences that build on one another and move in a clear direction.

Once, as part of my school's DEI team, I helped design a questionnaire about how race and gender had influenced students' experiences while in middle school. We surveyed 9th grade students because they could comment on their experiences throughout middle school without having to worry that their responses might somehow bias their teachers against them. We had our colleagues read anonymous quotes from the survey and discuss them using exploratory, pragmatic, and critical questions (similar to those in the bringback protocol in Chapter 3). Our colleagues gave us very positive feedback on this session—and then never had an opportunity to reevaluate their practices based on what they'd learned.

In working with other schools, I've noticed that this happens a lot: a great meeting begins work that never continues. From talking to teachers and leaders, I've learned that this is common with DEI work, but I've seen discussions of writing across the content areas, curriculum mapping, progressive pedagogy, STEAM, and authentic assessments begin and begin again as if teachers were trapped in a school-oriented version of the movie *Groundhog Day*.

Although leaders might intend to resume these conversations—and turn toward the work that brings deep and lasting change—something always seems to get in the way, and by the time a topic becomes the priority again, it's been so long and there's been so much turnover that the faculty must return to square one. Teachers find this cycle frustrating and start to feel like the only reason they talk about these topics at all is because they're trendy—or worse, because an administrator wants to be able to say it was covered.

I know how cynical that sounds, and there will be times when leaders *must* put certain initiatives aside to focus on an emergency. You can probably think of recent local or global situations that would rightly displace a professional learning event, but if the topic truly matters, then it merits sustained consideration. Ultimately, if professional learning itself matters, then it should be sustained.

Routinizing Professional Learning

The simplest way to make PD feel like part of a larger whole is to choose a structure you think will work well and make it a regular routine. For example, a language department could use the bringback protocol at their first meeting of every month; a 3rd grade team could do intervision once a semester; a diversity committee could host a lunchtime toolbox share series on Wednesdays in March; or a school could hold teacher-led workshops on in-service days. Eventually, these professional learning events will become rituals that orient teachers to where they are in the school year and who they are as a group.

If you routinize professional learning, then you need to protect that time. There will always be something more urgent: struggling students, falling test scores, a jeopardized budget, or a community event. You should use your best judgment about when to cancel a PD session to address a crisis.

In other cases, it might be appropriate—and even beneficial—to connect the session's content to the emergent problem. Environmentalist John Muir wrote, "When we try to pick out anything by itself, we find it hitched to everything else in the Universe" (2004, p. 87). How might the problem on everyone's mind be hitched to the topic of the professional learning event? Could that learning be part of a solution to the problem? Even if it isn't, how might participating in the event help teachers develop skills and relationships that better equip them to handle the problem? Making connections such as these can help you address emergent issues while also continuing the PD routine— again, if it makes sense to do so.

Creating Professional Learning Units

A *unit* is a time-bound set of interconnected learning tasks that work together to promote deeper conceptual understanding or more skillful performance. Many (if not most) teachers create units to help their students envision a larger learning goal. Each lesson builds on the last, and all lessons build toward an end product—whether that product is a tangible piece of work or just the knowledge learners have attained. For our purposes, the learners in question are teachers, the lessons are PD events, the concept they're studying is one of professional importance, and their skillful performance ultimately benefits students.

A professional learning unit, then, is a time-bound set of interconnected PD events that work together to help teachers understand education concepts more deeply and use their knowledge more skillfully to benefit students. The remainder of this chapter discusses two ways to create meaningful professional learning units.

Inquiry-Based PD Units

One way to create a sense of cohesiveness among different professional learning events is to integrate them into a project. All teachers, individually or in groups, create a meaningful product, and all professional learning activities help them visualize, make, or refine that product.

Imagine that a middle school faculty wants to use their websites as more effective teaching tools. Teachers might use the Exemplar Study protocol (page 52) to discover how colleagues use their websites especially well, attend peer-led workshops to learn how to incorporate particular tools and features into their own sites, and work in intervision groups to visit one another's websites and give feedback.

These activities aren't isolated events; they're part of a coordinated plan for teachers to learn how to use their websites more effectively. Figure 4.1 shows a plan for the website redesign project. Figures 4.2 and 4.3 show more examples of project-based PD unit plans.

FIGURE 4.1

Sample PD Unit Plan for a Website Redesign Project

Assignment: *Update your website so it serves as a more effective teaching tool.*

Week(s)	Grouping	Meeting
1	Grade-level teams	EXEMPLAR STUDY: Teachers examine specific teachers' websites.
2–6	Individuals	Teachers have dedicated time to plan and create their websites. Members of the technology team are available to provide support.
2–3	Self-selected groups	OPTIONAL WORKSHOPS: Faculty and staff members show their colleagues how to incorporate particular features and tools into a website.
4–5	Trios assigned within grade levels but across subjects	INTERVISION GROUPS: Teachers visit one another's virtual spaces to give and receive feedback.

Source: Copyright 2021 by Lauren Porosoff.

Notice that each sample schedule uses some, but not all, of the formats described in Chapter 3 and that any format can be used just once or multiple times during a unit. You can revise any format to meet your faculty's needs so they can complete the project successfully. For example, intervision usually means visiting one another's classrooms, but it can also mean visiting one another's websites. Finally, you can provide time for teachers to do background reading or simply work on the project.

Setting Teachers Up for Successful Projects

Projects demand significant time and effort, and the outcome is something that matters. Out of respect for the work teachers put in, and the important product that results, we can position all teachers to complete professional projects successfully by providing them with the following resources.

FIGURE 4.2

Sample PD Unit Plan for a Multicultural Curriculum Revision Project

Assignment: *Redesign a unit so it more effectively and equitably incorporates the perspectives of people in a historically marginalized group.*

Week(s)	Grouping	Meeting
1	Grade-level teams	TOOLBOX SHARES: Grade-level team members share their responses to the question *How do we affirm multiple experiences and perspectives in our curriculum?*
2–4	Self-selected groups	WORKSHOPS: Teachers whose lessons, assignments, and units exemplify excellent multicultural curriculum design present to their peers.
5	Subject-area departments	BRINGBACK: Teachers read the chapter "Adapting Curriculum for Multicultural Classrooms" from *Affirming Diversity* (Nieto & Bode, 2017) and discuss how to apply concepts from the reading to teaching their subject (e.g., "What does multicultural curriculum look like in math?").
6	Self-selected groups	COUNCILS: Based on what they learned from the Nieto and Bode reading, teachers bring *How can I* questions to groups of colleagues (e.g., *How can I make this project about leaders of the Industrial Revolution better acknowledge multiple experiences and perspectives?*).
7–8	Trios assigned across grade levels and subjects	INTERVISION GROUPS: Teachers observe one another teaching lessons redesigned to center historically marginalized experiences and perspectives. They discuss what they learned from these observations.

An earlier version of this unit plan appeared in the author's "Systems vs. Heaps: Aligning Professional Development to School Values," *Independent School, 74*(1), pp. 110–114.

A clear assignment. An assignment statement tells teachers what they'll ultimately do with their learning. For the project in Figure 4.1, the assignment was "Update your website so it serves as a more effective teaching tool." Here are more examples for project-based PD units:

- Working as an interdisciplinary team, plan an overnight trip for students in your grade level that connects to the curriculum in at least one subject and that teaches community stewardship.

FIGURE 4.3		
Sample PD Unit Plan for a Classroom Management Project		
Assignment: *Write a classroom management plan that is restorative, trauma informed, and culturally responsive.*		
Week(s)	Grouping	Meeting
1–3*	Randomly assigned groups	BRINGBACKS: Teachers meet three times with the same group to read and discuss selections from the following books: • *Better Than Carrots or Sticks: Restorative Practices for Positive Classroom Management* (Smith, Fisher, & Frey, 2015) • *The Trauma-Sensitive Classroom: Building Resilience with Compassionate Teaching* (Jennings, 2018) • *"These Kids Are Out of Control": Why We Must Reimagine "Classroom Management" for Equity* (Milner, Cunningham, Delale-O'Connor, & Kestenberg, 2018)
4	Grade-level teams	WORKSHOP: Instructional leaders show teachers how to write a classroom management plan.
5–7	Individuals	Teachers have dedicated time to write their classroom management plans. Members of the leadership, wellness, and DEI teams circulate and provide support.
8**	Grade-level teams	TOOLBOX SHARE: Grade-level team members share their responses to the question *How do we use our classroom management plans?*

* These sessions occur over three months. Between sessions, teachers are encouraged to reflect, read beyond the assigned selections, and discuss their readings informally.

** This session occurs two months after the classroom management plans are written so teachers have time to implement them.

Source: Copyright 2021 by Lauren Porosoff.

- Identify, adapt, and implement an academic learning routine that addresses a social, psychological, or physical need your students have.
- Make an online curriculum map that helps colleagues understand how you integrate STEM skills into your course.

An assignment statement not only helps teachers understand their task but also helps the leader create a unit plan. Imagine that an elementary school faculty is about to do the STEM mapping project. Teachers will need to (1) examine and analyze the middle school maps so they can use them as models for their own, (2) define what they mean by *STEM skills,* (3) determine how they integrate STEM skills into their curricula, (4) learn how to use the online mapping software, (5) make the maps, and (6) get feedback so they know their maps successfully communicate how they integrate STEM skills. Depending on how much time the leader can devote to this project and the teachers' prior knowledge, the school could spend part of a meeting, an entire meeting, or several meetings working through any given step. Whatever teachers need to do to complete the project, you need to ensure they *can* do. Your job becomes curating a series of professional learning events that builds teachers' capacity to complete the project successfully.

A list of criteria for excellence. If teachers are to complete the project successfully, they'll need to know what *success* means, based on what the school community values. Listing criteria helps teachers know what to strive for. The list also helps *you* notice what matters most so you can allocate time accordingly: the more important a particular criterion, the more time you should devote to ensuring teachers can meet it.

Multiple models of excellent work. Teachers need to see examples of work of the type they're being asked to create so they can visualize the end products of their own work. They could use the Exemplar Study protocol (see page 52) to help them consider the models, or they could simply look at the models so they have an image of completed work in mind.

Dedicated work time to reach the expected level of quality. To create excellent work products, teachers need time to learn new concepts and skills, generate drafts or versions, get feedback, make revisions, use what they've made, and reflect on the process.

Creating Inquiry-Based PD Units

Another way to create cohesiveness among professional learning events is to frame them as contributing to a sustained inquiry. In an inquiry, a question guides teachers as they explore a particular topic. Each learning event helps teachers expand or qualify how they understand the topic.

Imagine that a high school assistant principal constantly sees articles, blogs, and books about trauma-informed practices. When he mentions the term at lunch one day, a teacher says, "But we're not allowed to know the details of our students' trauma histories. Maybe you could give us more information so we could teach them better." Another teacher counters that children's home lives are their private business and that teachers shouldn't have to be therapists. "I feel for them," she says, "but those kids belong in an alternative education environment. We're just not set up for them here."

The AP just listens, taking mental notes of the misunderstandings he hears. From what he's read, he knows that being trauma informed doesn't mean knowing every personal detail about each child. He also knows that some of the teachers at the school are great at responding to children who have experienced trauma—without knowing those details and without acting as unlicensed therapists.

The AP decides to create a professional learning inquiry, using the question *What would it truly mean for us to be trauma informed?* Back in his office, he starts scrolling through his Twitter feed looking for some of the articles he's seen about trauma-informed practices. He figures he'll start by having each teacher choose one of three or four different articles and use the bringback protocol to have discussions with others who read the same article. Depending on what emerges from those discussions, he could then have teachers repeat the protocol with more articles, ask those who already use trauma-informed practices to offer workshops, invite teachers to present their questions about using trauma-informed practices to councils of their peers, or create intervision groups so teachers can observe one another using trauma-informed practices.

Using Essential Questions

To begin planning an inquiry-based PD unit, you first need to write what Grant Wiggins and Jay McTighe (2005) call an essential question. An essential question asks about a concept, process, or phenomenon that deserves teachers' attention throughout the unit. Just as we can develop essential questions about the material we teach to students, we can develop essential questions about teaching, learning, students, and systems.

Wiggins and McTighe argue that questions are essential when they point to "core ideas and inquiries within a discipline" and help learners "make sense of important but complicated ideas, knowledge, and know-how" (2005, p. 109). However, the ideas we deem "core" or "important" depend on our values. Within any group of educators, you'll often find at least some consensus around what they consider core and important because some set of commonly held values brought the group together in the first place. Any question a group considers essential will reflect that group's values. The following examples of essential questions reflect the values of the teachers who created them. Which ones reflect yours?

- What if we assigned authentic writing more often in our different classes?
- How might we use new digital tools to enhance learning? When might these tools interfere with learning?

- How would changing our school schedule affect our students and our work?
- What would it truly mean for us to be *trauma informed?*
- What does scholar Bettina L. Love (2019) mean by *abolitionist teaching*? What would it take to make our teaching abolitionist?

Even with these examples—and many more, which you can find online by searching for *essential question* along with an education key phrase such as *trauma informed* or *writing across the curriculum*—you might struggle to write an essential question to guide your faculty's professional learning. If so, you wouldn't be alone. When Wiggins and McTighe (2005) revised *Understanding by Design* for its second edition, they had to do "more painstaking back-and-forths of drafts of [their chapter on essential questions] than were necessary for any other part of the revision" because they "saw an inconsistency between the original account and widespread practice" (p. vii).

If you search online for essential questions about any given topic, you'll probably find questions that seem dull, confusing, wordy, insignificant, or vague. Ultimately, how good your question sounds matters less than how well it serves three critical functions: stimulating teachers' curiosity, raising the level of discourse, and providing a direction for the unit.

Stimulating Teachers' Curiosity

When we hear questions that excite us, we feel motivated to seek answers. By contrast, if the question feels irrelevant, confusing, or otherwise off-putting, we might not bother pursuing it. One way to spark teachers' natural curiosity is to write a question that reflects their experiences—perhaps by inviting their stories, challenging their assumptions, or pointing to a problem they've identified but haven't yet been able to solve. For example, asking "What would it truly mean for us to be trauma informed?" suggests that these teachers have tried to support students with trauma histories (and might have success stories to share), and that they need to confront some of their own thinking and take different actions.

You can also elicit their interest by asking teachers to imagine an alternative to their current set of experiences, doing what museum consultant Leslie Bedford (2016) calls "working in the subjunctive mood" (p. 14). Bedford explains that during the time when she was learning to make exhibitions, she was also learning the Spanish language, and "like many English speakers, [she] found the subjunctive mood intriguing but challenging" (p. 15) because it expresses possibilities—or *what-ifs*—in a way that doesn't quite translate into English. Bedford wanted to capture this mood of *What if?* when designing exhibitions so viewers would imagine what *could* be instead of absorbing knowledge about what *is*. You don't have to use the subjunctive case, but you can try writing an essential question that gets teachers to wonder, "What if . . . ?"

Raising the Level of Discourse

As an education leader, you probably already know about "A Revision of Bloom's Taxonomy" (Krathwohl, 2002), which distinguishes lower-level thinking (such as recognizing correct answers, recalling basic information, and comprehending texts and situations) from higher-level thinking, which includes practical application, critical analysis, and imaginative synthesis. If, for example, teachers were to explore trauma-informed practice, we'd want them to do more than memorize a definition of *trauma*, describe fight-flight-freeze responses, and correctly answer questions about coping strategies. We'd want them also to apply their understanding of trauma when observing one another's classrooms, assess how well homework policies take trauma into account, and imagine classroom routines that would help students feel safe. A good essential question stimulates deeper, broader, and more creative thinking about the unit topic.

Providing a Direction for the Unit

An essential question not only names an important topic but also suggests a direction for exploring it. The question *What would it truly mean for us to be trauma informed?* contains an important topic (trauma) and a reason for learning about it. It requires teachers to define *trauma informed* in a specific context and consider how a more sophisticated understanding of student trauma might shape interactions, policies, and programs. Precisely because the topic is so vast—and because so many activities could count as professional learning—you need some way to articulate a direction for considering it. The essential question then serves as a gatekeeper for unit content and activities: whatever doesn't advance the inquiry doesn't belong in the unit.

Planning Inquiry-Based Units

Inquiries don't lend themselves to advance planning the way projects do. A project-based unit has a predetermined outcome: successful completion of the work product. You backward plan a project to get to that outcome (by scheduling time for teachers to explore new ideas and strategies, create and refine their work product, get feedback, and reflect on their process). Although projects are notoriously iterative—full of attempts, mistakes, and do-overs—you have an outcome in mind and can select a series of events that lead toward that outcome.

By contrast, an inquiry-based unit has no outcome other than engaging in the inquiry itself. You can backward plan a project because it has a destination, but inquiries don't. They do have a direction, as articulated in the essential question. You can forward plan an inquiry from that essential question, and although you might have possible next steps in mind, you can change course depending on where the inquiry takes you. If you *do* have an outcome or destination in mind, then your unit isn't an inquiry; it's a project.

Because an inquiry can begin with any professional learning event that meaningfully addresses the essential question, you're best off starting with a format that positions all teachers as equals, such as a toolbox share that taps into everyone's existing knowledge or a bringback that familiarizes the entire community with new content. From there, you can plan another event that either builds on expertise or addresses learning goals that emerge. In other words, some teachers will show themselves as experts and others as learners, so it will make sense for them to be positioned as such in the next round of professional learning events during the inquiry.

Figure 4.4 has a flowchart you can use to help you plan a series of learning events for an inquiry-based professional learning unit, depending on the expertise and needs that emerge after each round.

Another way to begin an inquiry is with a learning event that involves relatively little risk. Figure 4.5 shows the six peer-to-peer PD formats from Chapter 3, arranged on a heat map based on how much vulnerability they invoke. Darker squares represent more vulnerability, and lighter squares represent less. When one person is positioned as different or distinct from the others (such as when they present a workshop), they become more vulnerable than when everyone is positioned as equals, such as in a toolbox share.

Also, when we set out to grow or improve, we make ourselves vulnerable by sharing what we can't and don't know how to do. Although the highest achievers got to their level of performance precisely because they got feedback and support, help-seeking can still trigger feelings of *I'm not good enough*. Then again, positioning ourselves as experts can invoke vulnerability, too. We might feel anxious that we'll forget to say something important, confuse or bore our audience, not know the answer to a question, make a mistake, or come off as arrogant. That's why the vulnerability heat map gets darker on *both* sides. If you're not sure how to begin an inquiry-based PD unit, start with

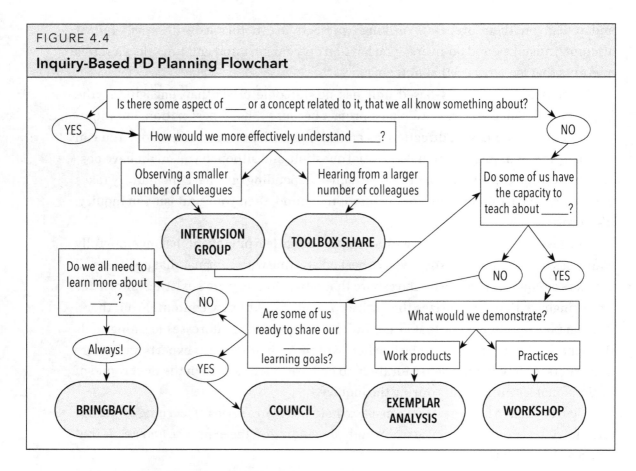

FIGURE 4.4

Inquiry-Based PD Planning Flowchart

formats that invoke less vulnerability. As you continue to plan events that address the essential question, stick with lower-risk formats until your faculty seems ready, and then you can try riskier ones.

Choosing a PD Unit Type

Project- and inquiry-based units can make professional learning more cohesive, yet both unit types present challenges. The biggest challenge of an inquiry-based unit is that without a specific outcome to work toward, teachers might wonder what will result from their efforts. If you sense that your faculty (not to mention your supervisor) will want a visible and measurable outcome of their work, then you might want to go with a project.

The biggest challenge of a project-based unit is that it might invoke deficit thinking. When we ask practicing teachers to create something new, they might get the message that whatever they're already doing isn't good enough. For example, some teachers might understand a request to make a unit more multiculturally inclusive to mean that their existing units aren't inclusive enough. In other words, the unit they'd write would be *better* than the one they already have—so they might interpret that we think their current work is *bad*. If we ask some teachers to offer their expertise, such as in a workshop or exemplar study, then participants might get the message that the experts are doing it *right* and they therefore must be doing it *wrong*.

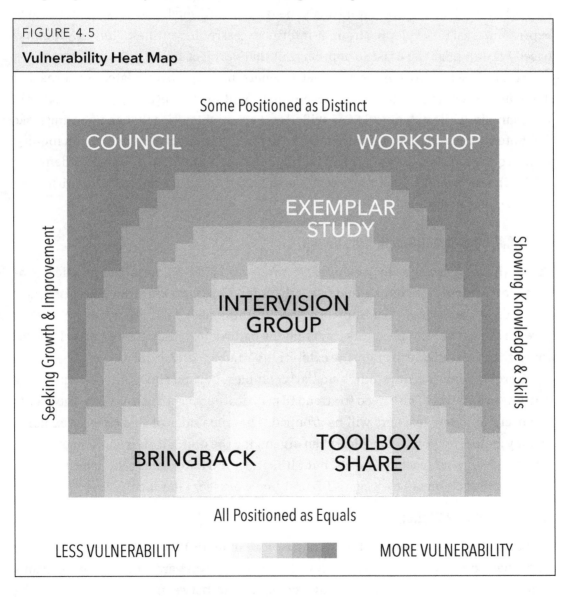

FIGURE 4.5

Vulnerability Heat Map

Some Positioned as Distinct

COUNCIL   WORKSHOP

EXEMPLAR
STUDY

Seeking Growth & Improvement

Showing Knowledge & Skills

INTERVISION
GROUP

TOOLBOX
SHARE

BRINGBACK

All Positioned as Equals

LESS VULNERABILITY   MORE VULNERABILITY

We can look to improve even if our current work is good, and we can learn from other people even if we already know a lot. But some teachers might become defensive if asked to work on a project. And some teachers might not be ready to create something new, especially in an area they're only beginning to learn about.

If you think your team isn't ready to get an assignment and needs to do some exploring first, then an inquiry-based unit might be more appropriate than a project. After—or even during—the inquiry, teachers might start to suggest projects themselves. For example, after learning what it means to be trauma informed, teachers might begin to express interest in developing trauma-informed classroom routines. Thus, any inquiry-based PD unit might give rise to another unit that's project-based.

Similarly, while working on a project, teachers might discover related concerns that don't directly contribute to the project but that could shape a future inquiry-based unit. For example, while mapping STEM skills, teachers might notice that engineering tasks promote student creativity. For their next PD unit, these teachers might do an inquiry, using a question such as "How might we use engineering tasks to promote student creativity in our classes?" Just as projects can give rise to future inquiries, inquiries can give rise to future projects.

Practical Considerations in Unit Design

In addition to creating a story, exhibition curators must take a variety of practical concerns into account, including budgets, schedules, object preservation, ease of maintenance, and aesthetics. Curators also need to think about the attendees not just as viewers but as people: "If visitors can't find the bathroom, if they get lost or feel unwelcome, they are unlikely to enjoy the exhibitions" (Lubar, 2017, p. 189).

A professional learning unit is similarly complex. Beyond choosing and sequencing learning events, you'll also need to attend to practical concerns such as when the events will occur and how teachers will be grouped. The remainder of this chapter explores five key factors for you to consider when organizing the unit. I'll offer some suggestions for how to support teachers' needs, but ultimately, you know your school best and are therefore best equipped to design a PD unit that works for your faculty.

Pacing for Differentiation

Some teachers might be able to map STEM skills in 15 minutes, whereas others might need a one-on-one review of how the mapping software works or more examples of how to articulate skills. Leave enough time between professional learning events for teachers to plan, ask questions, exchange ideas, try new strategies, and seek help—and for you to respond to any emergent needs. Spreading out PD events also means you can use intervening meetings for other purposes.

Sending Follow-up Resources

Any topic substantial enough for a professional learning unit probably has loads of associated resources available that could help teachers learn more. Sometimes, PD providers send out resources before an event so teachers can come prepared with greater stores of background knowledge.

The problem with sending out resources in advance is that, very often, teachers won't read them. One of the schools where I used to work held a summer Progressive Teaching Institute, which served to introduce newly hired teachers to the school's philosophy and as an optional professional learning experience for continuing teachers. For several years, the institute's planning committee sent out a book in which educator Mabel Goodlander (1921) wrote about the school's progressive curriculum and pedagogy. It made sense to ask teachers to read about how their school enacted progressive education almost a century prior and compare that to today. One year at my table of 10 teachers, only two had read Goodlander's book. The rest hadn't—not because they didn't care about their school or progressive teaching but because they all had plenty to do in the weeks before school started, and they hadn't experienced anything to activate their interest in the school's progressive history.

Instead of assigning prereadings, try sending annotated lists of follow-up resources—links to articles, videos, podcasts, webinars, and books that address the PD unit topic or (if possible) the specific subtopic of that PD event. For each link, include a brief comment that explains what it's about or how it connects to that day's learning. That way, teachers who want to explore the topic further have ways to do so. You'll also send the message that there is always more to learn.

Creating Successful Groupings

During a professional learning unit, teachers have multiple opportunities to work in groups. If teachers learn within existing groups, such as discipline-based departments or grade-based teams, then their conversations might carry over into other work the group does together. Teachers might also be more likely to take creative risks and share personal experiences within a group of people they already know well.

However, PD units create opportunities for teachers to learn from and with colleagues they *don't* typically work alongside. Also, some teachers might be less likely to take risks and share stories with people in their department or team, especially if they feel marginalized or unsafe within that group. For these reasons, consider mixing up the groupings from unit to unit or even from activity to activity within a unit. One way to make PD groups is to deliberately remix existing groups so teachers of different subjects and grade levels can build new relationships and get fresh perspectives on their work.

Another way to make PD groups is to give teachers some choice as to the session they attend or the group itself. If different groups are doing different things—such as discussing different articles about trauma or attending one of several concurrent workshops on designing multicultural curriculum—then you can have teachers choose their sessions based on their professional goals and interests.

If the groups are all doing the same thing, then give a choice about the group itself. For example, if the entire faculty is working in intervision trios, or if several teachers are presenting questions in councils, then consider giving teachers some choice as to who's in their groups. However, if you simply tell teachers to organize themselves into groups, they might choose colleagues they already know well—and therefore miss an opportunity to learn from someone new. Worse, teachers might replicate the social cliques and power imbalances that already exist within the institution.

To balance the need for teacher agency with the goal of building a stronger learning community, you can make the groups but send out a survey to ask teachers to list the names of 10 colleagues with whom they'd like to be grouped. With lists that long, you should be able to make groups so everyone works with at least one colleague they asked for. To give yourself flexibility, say that you'll try to honor requests but won't promise anything.

When you send the survey, attach a list of all the faculty and staff members at your school and ask everyone to consider what they might learn from observing each colleague—especially those with whom they don't typically work. You can also include a place for teachers to indicate that they'd be happy to work with anyone.

Assigning Roles

Give different teachers different roles from one learning event to another so the usual suspects aren't always the ones showcasing their work. If five teachers offer their work for exemplar study in January, then a *different* five teachers could offer workshops in February. If the chairperson selects an article for her department's first bringback, then a new member could select the next article the department reads. Any particular event will position some people as learners and others as experts—or everyone as a learner or expert—but over the course of an entire unit, different teachers should have a chance to occupy these roles so everyone can ultimately learn *and* contribute.

Celebrating Growth

One school where I taught had a sunshine committee that collected a few dollars from each teacher and used that money to buy a sheet cake and a card when a faculty or staff member got married or had a baby. During one of these celebrations, a colleague who'd recently completed her master's degree asked why only certain life events merited sheet cake. As a school—a *learning* institution—why couldn't we celebrate learning?

To be clear, you don't have to buy a sheet cake every time a faculty member finishes a PD unit (although there isn't really a bad time for cake), but ask yourself whether your school celebrates milestones. If so, which milestones do you celebrate? How? If you already have celebratory traditions, consider extending them to mark professional learning. Alternatively, ask teachers how they'd like to celebrate. (I recommend sheet cake.)

Learning from Learners

Writing a unit plan doesn't mean you have to stick to it. In fact, sometimes it's better to deviate from your plan. Teachers certainly will. Steven Lubar (2017) explains that even though some museums literally "put footprints on the floor to show visitors the path to follow" (p. 157), people often don't follow that path. On the contrary, visitors are "free-range learners," there to "pique and satisfy their curiosity . . . not to memorize facts or imbibe a curator's narrative" (p. 160).

Professional learning is the same. Even if you carefully plan out a sequence of learning events that proceeds logically from a question or leads logically toward an outcome, teachers come to these events with their own interests and goals. They might not follow the footprints on the floor, so to speak. Instead of seeing these behaviors as failures—ours because we didn't make the path clear enough, or teachers' because they refused to comply—we should *expect* teachers to bring their own agendas and creative interpretations to their learning. As curators, we can learn from them. Regardless of what we've planned, we can pay attention to what teachers actually do and remain flexible.

Onward

This chapter was about how to integrate peer-to-peer learning events into a meaningful and cohesive whole, either by using a particular PD structure repeatedly so it becomes a learning routine or by creating a professional learning unit. In Chapter 5, we'll learn how to assess PD events and units so we can meet teachers' needs as learners—and ultimately help them meet the needs of their students.

Make It Effective:
Assessing Professional Learning

As a teenager, I visited museums less often than I did as a little kid, but my friends and I still sometimes went. I can't say I personally played keep-away in the Temple of Dendur at The Metropolitan Museum of Art, but I know people who did. At the American Museum of Natural History, the room with the giant blue whale suspended from the ceiling was a great place to kiss your boyfriend if you had one, and the Hayden Planetarium was a preferred destination for my peers who were partaking in then-illegal substances. One of my friends said that the Guggenheim's main gallery (a marvelous feat of architecture that spirals from the top of the building to the bottom so you can look at the art as you curl your way down) was also a great place to skateboard. He claimed to have gotten in trouble doing it, but I think he made up the whole thing. Still, we enjoyed misbehaving at museums—or even the *idea* of misbehaving at museums. We were rebellious teenagers, so where better to assert our (somewhat misguided) agency than these places that told the world what higher culture was supposed to mean?

It's hard to picture the curators of these exhibits taking interest in such shenanigans, except maybe to be annoyed that we weren't paying the right kind of attention to the content—let alone using them as evidence that their work was successful. After spending so much time thoughtfully caring for, selecting, arranging, displaying, and explaining the items, I'd think curators would be more interested in visitors actually learning about said items than skateboarding past them.

However, according to John Falk (2016), whose enviable job title is professor of free-choice learning, only a small minority of museum visitors go with a specific learning objective. Others go because they're broadly curious about the museum's content, they see the museum as a place where they can entertain people (such as children, out-of-town guests, or a date), they find that museum-going relaxes and restores them, or they just want to have the experience of going to a museum.

Falk suggests that we "stop thinking about museum exhibitions and content as fixed and stable entities designed to achieve singular outcomes and instead think of them as intellectual resources capable of being experienced and used in different ways for multiple, and equally valid, purposes" and that visitors derive meaning "largely shaped by short-term personal, identity-related needs and interests rather than by the goals and intentions of the museum's staff" (2016, p. 35).

Although Falk is writing about environments where most visitors spend leisure time—not workplaces—his suggestions apply just as well to professional learning. As a school leader, you surely have your own objectives when you curate PD, but teachers are individuals who bring their own needs and interests to their professional learning, and any particular learning event or unit can be experienced in multiple valid ways. Just as people visit museums with their own ideas about what a good experience could be, teachers come to PD with their own ideas about what makes the experience meaningful. Whether *we* achieved our objectives is only one way to define effectiveness.

In this chapter, we're going to look at different ways of defining *effective* professional learning and how you, as a PD curator, can assess and support the effectiveness of PD events.

Defining Effectiveness in Professional Learning

To understand how we might define *effectiveness,* let's revisit the example of a teacher presenting a workshop on flipped classrooms (Bergmann & Sams, 2012). Early in his session, the teacher might state learner objectives—for example, that participants will be able to (1) describe the strengths and challenges of flipped classrooms, and (2) create their own flipped classroom videos. Like any participatory experience, this one is only partially in the presenter's hands; participants have the power to engage and learn or to disengage and come away with little new knowledge. Still, if his colleagues can describe the strengths and challenges of flipped classrooms and create their own videos, we can call this workshop a success.

Since this was an in-house professional learning experience, the teacher-presenter might also have a third objective: authentically connecting with his colleagues. This isn't a *learning* objective; it's a *collegial* objective. His colleagues, in turn, might have an objective of supporting him. If the presenter shares his experiences, and if his colleagues listen actively, ask questions, have small-group discussions, and otherwise participate—even if they have no intention of flipping their own classrooms—then the workshop has fulfilled its collegial objectives.

A second way to define *effectiveness* is if the workshop feels satisfying and meaningful to participants. Teachers might show up for the workshop with their own ideas about what constitutes effective PD. Some might be curious about any new education practice. Some might like spending time with specific colleagues who are also attending. Some might enjoy challenges such as making a video. Some might appreciate opportunities for group conversation, whereas others might prefer individual reflection time. Some might want to come away with a concrete plan they can use next week; others might want to dig into the underlying theory and research. Some might find it important that everyone in the room has a voice; others might want to hear only from those with the greatest expertise. Each of these teachers will feel differently about the workshop, depending on how well it satisfied their own needs, interests, and values.

Finally, the workshop might lead to unexpected changes in how teachers think, work, and interact. Maybe some attendees start thinking more about how to use their class time for deeper, more creative, and more collaborative work. Maybe two teachers happen to sit together, and during one of the turn-and-talks, they get an idea for a project they begin working on together. Maybe the presenter mentions a book about flipped classrooms, and one person starts browsing through related books and finds one about assessment that ends up transforming the way she tracks student progress. Maybe one teacher ends up using the workshop as an example of peer-to-peer professional learning in a book she writes five years later.

Even if not a single teacher starts using the flipped classroom method, the workshop might still have a profoundly important influence on how teachers approach their work. And if the workshop isn't an isolated event but part of a coordinated peer-to-peer professional learning system, then we might begin to see changes in how teachers approach their work, one another, and themselves. That is, in-house PD can change faculty culture into one of growth, leadership, appreciation, and connection.

We've now seen three ways to define *effectiveness* when curating PD:

- The PD *fulfills its objectives,* including learning objectives and collegial objectives.
- The PD *feels meaningful and satisfying to participants,* based on what matters to them.

- The PD *promotes a positive faculty culture* of continuous growth, flexible leadership, wide appreciation, and authentic connection.

The remainder of this chapter will describe ways to assess in-house PD according to these three distinct definitions of *effectiveness* and how you can support the ongoing effectiveness of professional learning at your school.

Assessing Whether PD Fulfilled Its Objectives

The protocols in this book proceed from the assumption that just having teachers share, listen, and explore together is enough. If you've created an inquiry-based unit, then perhaps the only outcome you're looking for is engagement in that inquiry. If you've created a project, then perhaps the only outcome you're looking for is successful completion of that work product. That said, you might be interested in assessing the extent to which the teachers you lead have achieved specific learning or collegial objectives.

Anytime we design a learning event, for students or for teachers, we have some set of goals in mind. In broadest terms, our goals involve expanding the learner's repertoire—that is, adding to their storehouse of knowledge and tools so they can understand an idea more fully or do something better than before.

In schools, we put a lot of energy into creating, articulating, and following learning objectives (*Students will be able to . . .*). We write learning objectives on the board, check throughout lessons to ensure students are achieving them, reteach material if students don't achieve the objectives, test for them, and consider ourselves and our students successful if and when the test scores are sufficiently high. Even arguments about engaging students in a lesson often hinge on the outcome of that engagement: they'll retain more information and produce better work. It's as if having an exciting intellectual conversation, sharing related personal experiences, imagining, speculating, asking questions, or otherwise making meaningful use of students' time isn't enough of an end unto itself. We focus on outcomes, sometimes at the expense of the present moment.

When we assess adult learning—if we assess it at all—we tend to focus on the event itself, even if we have outcomes in mind. Let's imagine a conference presentation about how to support anxious students. The provider—maybe he's a clinical psychologist—shows a slide with a set of learning objectives: *Participants will be able to (1) teach students a variety of coping strategies, (2) implement supportive modifications at the classroom and building level, and (3) help students connect their assignments to their own values so that any anxiety they feel is worthwhile.*

He then proceeds through his presentation, which shows participants how to teach coping strategies, implement supportive modifications, and lead values work. But as any educator knows, there's a vast difference between leading someone through material and having that person actually learn it.

If the presenter were a professor working with preservice teachers, he might have created a task to assess their learning, such as having them role-play coping exercises, draw classroom floor plans that include supportive modifications for anxious students, or design a lesson that embeds values work into academic instruction. However, PD providers don't typically create tasks to assess practicing teachers' learning (nor should they; practicing teachers have enough to do). Instead, they send surveys.

The anxiety presenter could email a survey to participants asking questions such as *How prepared do you now feel to teach coping strategies? To use supportive modifications? To embed values work into academic instruction?* But when teachers are asked for feedback on PD, these are not the kinds of questions they usually get. More often, teachers are asked to rate different aspects of the event itself (for example, *On a scale of 1 to 10, how would you rate the presenter's preparedness? The accessibility of the material? The interactiveness of the presentation? The overall event?*). I have filled out many post-PD surveys, and I can't remember a single one that asked me whether I used the ideas that were presented or how the experience changed my thinking, practice, or relationships.

If you send a survey after a professional learning event, ask teachers about their learning. And because, alongside its learning objectives, in-house PD has a set of collegial objectives—to exchange ideas, explore together, listen to one another, ask questions, seek help, and build community—you should ask about those, too.

Let's imagine that a science department chair has organized a toolbox share using the question *How do we encourage science students to develop and pursue their own interests?* One teacher maintains a library of popular science books that connect to and extend beyond her curriculum. The chair is hoping that more teachers will create science libraries and, more generally, that more teachers will use one another's practices to encourage their students to develop and pursue science-related interests.

Figures 5.1, 5.2, and 5.3 all have example surveys that assess the effectiveness of in-house PD, with intentional variety in the question types. All three include learning objectives related to the event topics, as well as collegial objectives that matter to the

FIGURE 5.1
Sample Survey Assessing a Science Department Toolbox Share

To what extent are the following statements true for you?

	Very true	Somewhat true	Neither true nor false	Somewhat false	Very false
I learned about a practice I don't use and might now try.					
Everyone in the group had a chance to speak.					
Everyone in the group listened to one another.					
I had a follow-up conversation with a colleague about something that came up during the discussion.					
I sought out other opportunities to learn more about topics I heard about (such as by finding an article or book to read).					
What did you get out of this session?					
_____					
What did you contribute to this session?					
_____					

respective leaders. Instead of asking participants to rate the event itself, these surveys ask about how the event changed their actions or their capacity to take action.

When designing a survey, consider how much time it will take teachers to complete it. It's easier for teachers to check boxes than compose responses, and it's easier for you to analyze data from multiple-choice responses than read written ones. For your own sake as well as your teachers', limit the number of questions and try not to include more than two or three questions that require writing.

FIGURE 5.2

Sample Survey Assessing a Flipped Classroom Workshop

What would you say is the biggest advantage of using a flipped classroom model?

_____

What would you say is the biggest challenge in using a flipped classroom model?

_____

After the workshop, how interested are you in learning more about the flipped classroom model?

☐ I'm very interested.
☐ I'm somewhat interested.
☐ I've learned all I need for now.

To what extent did the workshop prepare you to use the flipped classroom model?

☐ I could use it now; I'd just need to create the video and lesson plan.
☐ I can picture it in my classroom, but I'd need support if I were to do it.
☐ I can't picture how to pull it off in my classroom.

What would help you feel more prepared to use the flipped classroom model?

☐ More examples of the flipped classroom model
☐ Help making videos
☐ Lesson ideas
☐ Classroom management strategies
☐ Feedback on my plans and materials
☐ Something else:_____

Regardless of whether you plan to use the flipped classroom model, to what extent do you agree or disagree with the following statements?

	Agree	Neither agree nor disagree	Disagree
One of the best ways for students to spend class time is to do challenging real-world work.			
One of the best ways for students to spend class time is to work collaboratively.			
Students should do their most challenging work in class where teachers can support them.			
When possible, students should learn new material at their own pace.			
Schools should provide students with all the tools and materials they need to complete assignments, regardless of *where* they complete their assignments.			

FIGURE 5.3

Sample Survey Assessing Intervision

As a result of either watching your colleagues teach or hearing what they have to say about your teaching . . .
What, if anything, will you *start* doing or do more of?

_____

What, if anything, will you *stop* doing or do less of?

_____

What will you *keep* doing, because it seems to be working well?

_____

Do you feel that at *least* one of your colleagues contributed to your professional learning during this process?
- ☐ Yes
- ☐ No
- ☐ Unsure

Do you feel you contributed to at *least* one of your colleagues' professional learning as a result of this process?
- ☐ Yes
- ☐ No
- ☐ Unsure

Do you feel closer to *at least* one of your colleagues as a result of this process?
- ☐ Yes
- ☐ No
- ☐ Unsure

When you collect survey data about professional learning events, it's up to you to decide what constitutes a *good* result. For the science department's toolbox share, is it enough that everyone *knows about* one another's practices, or do they have to actually use one? Is it enough that one or two teachers are trying something new, or does a majority of the department (or even the whole department) have to change? Are small changes enough, or do the changes have to be big?

Conversely, could the science department chair deem the toolbox share an effective professional learning experience if teachers simply described their practices and listened actively when their colleagues spoke? The answers to these questions all depend on values—the chair's, the department's, and the school community's.

Finally, surveys don't always yield helpful responses. Some teachers will tell you whatever they think will please you—especially if you're in a supervisory role. Even if they're trying to be honest and forthright, they might not notice, remember, or be able to describe changes in their behaviors. Therefore, their responses will depend on how you word the question, how they happen to feel about their work and colleagues on the day they get the survey, and how much they like filling out surveys (Schwarz & Oyserman, 2001). Still, a survey provides *some* information, and if nothing else, it shows teachers that you care about their experiences—especially if you later report back about the survey results and explain how you're using them to guide future decisions.

One big advantage of in-house PD is that you have a continuing relationship with the people for whom you've curated. You could visit a museum and never go again, and you could attend a conference session without so much as introducing yourself to the presenter, let alone have contact with them beyond that hour. But if you curate PD for your faculty, you get to see them every day afterward. Therefore, you have access to something that museum curators and career PD providers don't have: direct observations of how effectively the recipients use it. You don't have to rely only on surveys to find out how effective the PD was. You can see for yourself what teachers do with it.

Assessing Whether PD Felt Meaningful and Satisfying to Participants

Think back on some of your best learning experiences. What was one of the best professional learning experiences you've ever had? What was one of the best classroom learning experiences you had when you were a student? What was one of the best learning experiences you've had outside a school setting? Take a minute or two to jot down what made each learning experience so good.

When considering what makes a learning experience meaningful, people sometimes think of the outcome, or what happened *as a result of* that experience, such as discovering useful lesson-planning strategies or gaining the confidence to cook a vegan dinner. Sometimes, people think a learning experience is meaningful because of the process, or what happened *during* the experience, such as bonding with colleagues or experimenting with new recipes.

As a leader, you have a set of objectives in mind when you design PD—just as you expect your faculty to have objectives in mind when they design lessons and assignments. Alongside those expectations, teachers bring their own ideas of what makes professional learning effective. Assessing PD's effectiveness might mean determining how well the event fulfilled the objectives you had in mind. But it might *also* mean determining how meaningful and satisfying the event was for teachers—according to their own criteria.

The tool in Figure 5.4 has teachers identify factors that make professional learning experiences meaningful and satisfying to them. Based on those factors, they rate the PD event, explain why they assigned the ratings they did, and offer suggestions for how the event might have gotten a higher rating.

FIGURE 5.4

What Makes PD Meaningful?

Identify the three factors that are most important to you to make a professional learning experience meaningful and satisfying. You can choose from the following list or articulate your own criteria. Label your three factors *A, B,* and *C* for reference.

For me, PD is meaningful and satisfying when it is . . .

- *Inclusive.* Everyone has a chance to contribute.
- *Equitable.* Voices that tend to be marginalized are more amplified, and voices that tend to be dominant are less amplified.
- *Experiential.* Attendees learn how to do something for their work by trying it themselves.
- *Active.* Attendees have opportunities to get up and move around while they learn.
- *Collaborative.* Pairs or groups work together and help each other succeed.
- *Reflective.* Attendees have opportunities to consider their own experiences and practices in light of what's being taught.
- *Generative.* The session is "make and take" so attendees leave with something they've created and can use in their work.
- *Differentiated.* Individuals or groups do their own work, according to their needs or interests.
- *Practical.* The work easily translates into concrete action.
- *Intellectual.* Rather than providing easy answers, the session exposes questions, complexities, and hypotheses.
- *Playful.* The session presents new practices or ideas in fun or gamelike ways.
- *Exploratory.* The session provides opportunities for attendees to ask questions and make attempts.
- *Anti-biased.* The session promotes self-awareness, identity consciousness, perspective taking, and acting for justice.
- *Accessible.* The content is available in formats that are clear and easy for all attendees to understand and use.
- *Responsive.* The leader adapts to accommodate different people, circumstances, concerns, and needs.
- *Welcoming.* The leader has a warm demeanor and ensures everyone feels cared for.
- *Diverse.* The session brings together people from a wide variety of professional and sociocultural backgrounds.
- *Unifying.* Members of the group feel a sense of solidarity by the end.
- *Innovative.* The material is fresh, new, and different.
- *Transformative.* The ideas have an immediate and dramatic influence on attendees' work or thinking.
- *Embedded.* The session contributes to a larger, longer-term, and more comprehensive goal or vision.

Write the three factors you chose on the blank lines and respond to the resulting questions.

	Hardly			Somewhat				Very		
How [A]_____ was this PD event?	1	2	3	4	5	6	7	8	9	10

In what ways was this event [A]_____?

What would have made the event *more* [A]_____?

	Hardly			Somewhat				Very		
How [B]_____ was this PD event?	1	2	3	4	5	6	7	8	9	10

In what ways was this event [B]_____?

What would have made the event *more* [B]_____?

	Hardly			Somewhat				Very		
How [C]_____ was this PD event?	1	2	3	4	5	6	7	8	9	10

In what ways was this event [C]_____?

What would have made the event *more* [C]_____?

Because each teacher creates different criteria for what makes an event meaningful and satisfying, you can't average the ratings together, but you can look for patterns. If the ratings are high overall, then you know you've created an event that is meaningful and satisfying in many ways. If the ratings are mixed, then look to see *which* ratings are low, and try to make future events rate higher in those ways. For example, if the science department chair sees that the toolbox share got low ratings for *diverse*—if only because everyone in the room was a science teacher—then maybe next time she could ask the art department to participate.

You can also look to see *whose* ratings are low, and work with that person to make future events more satisfying for them. For example, if a workshop got high ratings from veteran teachers but low ratings from novices, then the principal could invite less-experienced teachers to help plan the next PD event. Low ratings don't necessarily mean the event was bad, but they do mean it didn't fulfill a need that group members find important. When you ask teachers to define their own criteria for evaluating their PD, you're showing that you care about what matters to them.

Assessing Whether PD Shifts Faculty Culture

If you do in-house PD regularly—as part of how your team or whole school runs—then it might begin to affect your faculty culture. How couldn't it? If culture is the sum total of a group's customs and beliefs, how could regular opportunities for teachers to learn together not begin to change the ways they relate to their work, their students, their colleagues, and themselves?

Over time, and maybe even right away, you might notice four cultural shifts:

- A shift toward *continuous learning,* as teachers actively clarify their goals and seek opportunities to grow and improve—not only at the PD events, but beyond.
- A shift toward *flexible leading,* so instead of relying on status conferred by one's role or seniority, people step into opportunities to head groups, develop initiatives, and guide thinking.
- A shift toward *wider appreciating,* as any knowledge that ultimately benefits students is considered to be valuable.
- A shift toward *authentic connecting* beyond preexisting affinities, as teachers discover common experiences and develop common values.

Cultural shifts are hard to track. Even the phrase *cultural shift* doesn't refer to any specific, concrete, countable set of things or behaviors in the real world. If you want to see the impact of in-house PD on faculty culture, you need an indicator. Try asking yourself one or more of the following questions:

- What kinds of conversations are teachers having in the lunchroom or lounge?
- Who contributes at meetings?
- What do you hear teachers say about their work? Do they say anything at all? Do they only use general evaluative language, like that a lesson was *good* or that the students' behavior was *terrible?* Or do they describe their work?
- When teachers are critical of something at school, what kinds of problems are they expressing concern about? Are they only stating problems or also suggesting solutions?
- What do you hear teachers say about one another?
- Who steps up—not only to present their expertise in formats such as workshops and exemplar studies but also to join committees and task forces?
- How much outside professional development are people requesting? For example, do you see any changes in the number of teachers asking to go to conferences, attend webinars, buy books or periodical subscriptions, or otherwise seek more learning?
- Who is requesting further professional development? Are the same PD junkies the ones asking for more, or do teachers who don't typically seek learning now ask for it?
- In what areas do teachers seek PD, through your in-house initiatives and beyond? Are teachers sticking with comfortable topics, or are they looking to branch out?
- Are teachers looking to share their work more widely, for example by presenting at conferences or writing articles?
- Who do you see having conversations? Do you see the same pairs or groups of teachers talking to each other, or are you starting to see new connections?

Even when we see evidence of cultural shifts (such as teachers having more and deeper conversations about their practice, stepping into leadership roles, sharing their work more widely, and developing more diverse connections), we can't say for sure that our PD activities caused them. Maybe teachers were already doing these things before the in-house PD program started, but we only started noticing them afterward. You'd need to take some baseline data—what teachers are doing before they start learning from and with one another—to see whether their behaviors change afterward. Even then, increased learning, leadership, appreciation, and connection could be the result of some other factor, such as hiring several energetic and talented new teachers. In other words, correlation is not causation; you might see that teachers' behavior has changed but not know why.

To infer causation, you'd need to use a research design such as a multiple-baseline study (Hayes, Barlow, & Nelson-Gray, 1999), which is when different groups experience the same interventions but at different points in time. This is possible, but it requires a gradual rollout of a standardized PD program (such as having a different department start doing toolbox shares each month) and systematic data collection to determine what, if any, changes the PD produced in each department's culture. Determining causation might be more work than it's worth, but even if you can't say with certainty that doing peer-to-peer professional learning is causing cultural shifts, you can still look for and celebrate these behaviors. More than that, you're in a position to *encourage* the changes you want to see!

The easiest and perhaps most important way to encourage positive change is simply to point it out. Sometimes, teachers feel like it doesn't matter how good they are at their jobs, how hard they work, or whether they implement the ideas they learned during professional development. Sometimes, it feels like the only thing that matters is that they show up and have their names checked off on an attendance sheet. Teachers want to feel as if their time and work made a difference—and that you, as the leader, notice that difference. Instead of holding people accountable for failing to implement new practices or even rewarding their successes, it's critical to simply notice their learning—and say what you notice.

You probably don't have the spare time to observe every teacher in your school, check every website, read every newsletter, and otherwise keep tabs on all the exciting goings-on in your school community. But anything you *can* do to find out how teachers are using the ideas and practices they've learned will enable you to comment on what you've noticed and ask relevant questions. If the science department just did a toolbox share on encouraging independent interests, the chair could do a walkthrough, see if any classes are doing independent reading, and then send those teachers a quick email: "Hey, I saw that your students were reading today! How's that going?" Watch physical spaces as well as virtual ones. If your teachers have websites or a social media presence, look there for evidence that they're using what they learned—and comment if they do. Keep your ears open for conversations about the topic teachers have studied and join the conversation if you can.

Praising teachers' efforts is fine, but making an observation or asking a question shows you're truly paying attention to what matters to *them* without adding your own judgment, even if that judgment is positive. When you show interest in what teachers are doing and care enough to find out more, you're giving one of the most precious resources you have: attention. Curiosity is generosity.

Supporting Strugglers and Stragglers

Approaching teachers with nonjudgmental curiosity about their new practices doesn't mean ignoring teachers who fall short. Let's imagine that after the science department's toolbox share about encouraging independent interests, the chair noticed that almost every class developed some sort of independent reading component. Some teachers asked students to contribute articles to read as part of their units, whereas others had students choose books about any science topic, which they'd read for a few minutes at the beginning of each class period. But Caleb found that whenever he tried to have his students read, they talked instead. And Janine expressed some skepticism about independent reading in science class because she feels that, although it's a worthwhile use of students' time, it belongs in English class. Both of these teachers might need support—Caleb because he's *struggling* to use his learning, and Janine because she's *straggling* behind the rest of the department. Teachers who struggle or straggle need different kinds of coaching, either from you or a mentor.

Psychologist Steven Hayes and his colleagues (Hayes, Gifford, Townsend, & Barnes-Holmes, 2001) describe two different kinds of problem solving: strategic and valuative. In strategic problem solving, we're aware of the outcome we want to achieve but not the actions that will help us achieve it. We're asking, *How can I do this?* or *What's the best way?* When I first developed osteoarthritis, I knew the outcome I wanted (less pain in my joints) but not the actions that would help me achieve it. So I went to my doctor, and she told me to stay better hydrated, exercise every day, and eat anti-inflammatory foods. She helped me with strategic problem solving by telling me some of the actions I could take to achieve the outcome I wanted.

When teachers *struggle* to implement professional practices, they know the outcomes they want but need help identifying actions that will achieve those outcomes. Caleb's department chair might offer suggestions for how he can keep his students quiet during independent reading time, for example by creating more comfortable spaces, expanding the classroom library to incentivize reading, or assigning seats and separating students who are more likely to distract each other. The chair could also have Caleb observe colleagues during their independent reading times to see what strategies they use to keep students quiet and on task. When you or someone else coaches a teacher who struggles, you can offer strategic problem-solving support.

In valuative problem solving, we're aware of possible actions we can take but not the outcome we want to achieve. We're wondering, *What do I truly want?* or *What matters most to me?* A simple example is looking at a menu. Is the deliciousness of a patty melt worth the heartburn, or should I choose the salad that's healthier and easier on my stomach? Big life decisions, such as whether to take a new job or get married, are valuative. We know what our options are, and we're trying to decide which outcome we want most.

When teachers *straggle* behind others in implementing new professional practices, they know the actions they can take but aren't sure which outcome they want most. Janine understands what independent reading is and how to do it, but she isn't sure it's worth the time in science class.

When coaching a teacher who straggles, you can offer valuative problem-solving support—but what exactly does that look like? Sometimes, when we think another person should change what they do, we try to convince them to make that change. You can probably imagine the science department chair trying to convince Janine of how great it would be if her kids read more science nonfiction.

As you might guess, trying to convince people often backfires. Another set of psychologists, William Miller and Stephen Rollnick (2013), explain that most people who contemplate change feel ambivalent about it; they see reasons to change and reasons not to. If we try to convince them to change, we're "siding with one voice on the person's internal committee" (p. 7), which prompts the person to voice the *other* side of the argument! Because "most people tend to believe themselves and trust their own opinions more than those of others," our getting them to "verbalize one side of an issue tends to move the person's balance of opinion in that direction" (p. 9). That is, the more we try to convince someone to take a certain action, the more likely they are to convince themselves *not* to take that action. If the department chair were to argue in favor of independent reading, Janine would most likely argue against it: independent reading would take too much time away from the science curriculum, it belongs in English class, there aren't enough well-written nonfiction books about science at her students' level, and so on. This is not because she's stubborn or difficult; it's just how ambivalence works.

Instead of making suggestions, try using the following strategies, adapted from Miller and Rollnick's work:

- **Summarize what the teacher is saying.** By saying back what the person is saying, you show you're listening, build trust, and provide an opportunity to correct any misunderstandings. If Janine expresses concern about the amount of time independent reading would take, the chair could say something like, "I hear you saying independent reading will take time, and the topics in your curriculum are too important to devote less time to."

- **Ask open-ended questions.** Your questions should be of the sort that a journalist or scientist might ask, as opposed to the closed or leading questions of the sort that an attorney might ask when cross-examining a witness. You're looking to evoke exploration and discovery, not defensiveness. Janine's chair could ask, "What happens when students first come into class?" or "What might happen if you added a list of recommended independent reading books to your next unit syllabus?" Questions such as these get teachers to consider new possibilities.

- **Validate the teacher's experience.** Although you might see this person as resistant (and maybe kind of a pain), that resistance comes from a particular set of personal and professional circumstances. Even if you don't agree with the decision this person is making in the present moment, you can still respect their past history, as well as the strengths they developed as a result. Janine's chair might say, "It sounds like you've spent a lot of time looking for nonfiction science books on your students' level, and it's been frustrating to find so few."

- **Reflect back common values.** Even if the teacher hesitates or outright refuses to adopt a new practice, their reasoning might go back to values you share. Janine wants her students to use their time wisely and learn deeply. In all likelihood, those are values her department chair also holds. Saying so would remind Janine that she and her chair are in this work together and that even if they disagree on the *how,* they have a common *why.*

- **Invite the teacher into further conversations.** You might not come to a satisfying resolution after one or even several discussions, but letting the teacher know you want to keep talking shows you care as much about maintaining a relationship as encouraging a particular action.

Supporting Teachers Who Excel

Sometimes in schools, only the people who struggle get attention. For both students and teachers, performing at a high level can mean getting ignored. But teachers who truly excel at implementing the ideas and practices they learn about also need your attention and support.

One administrator I used to work with called herself a *furtherer*. She said she wanted to help members of her faculty and staff build on their strengths, extend their influence, and become the best versions of themselves. For a teacher, going further might mean taking on a leadership role, becoming a mentor, or sharing work beyond the four walls of their school.

If you find teachers who are taking their work to the next level (say, by creating innovative systems for encouraging independent reading), you can help those teachers further their work by encouraging them to write about it or present it at conferences. Consider the following four potential purposes of teachers' writing or presentations:

- *Share and connect.* The teacher tells a story and invites others to understand, relate to, and learn from their experiences.
- *Inspire and instruct.* The teacher explains how and why they did something so others can do it too.
- *Critique and propose.* The teacher analyzes a problem they've encountered and offers a better alternative.
- *Apply and extend.* The teacher uses a story, image, or concept they encountered outside school to illuminate a problem or issue they encountered in school.

Let's imagine that after the science department toolbox share, one teacher develops an especially good classroom library of trade books about science. To get his work further into the world, he could post on social media about his students' book choices and their resulting insights (*share and connect*). He could blog about how to apply for funding to create a science classroom library (*inspire and instruct*). He could join a panel at the National Science Teaching Association's annual conference and describe how traditional science textbooks limit student interest, yet having students choose books to read independently fosters interest (*critique and propose*). Or he could submit a graphic to *AMLE Magazine,* which is published by the Association for Middle Level Educators, showing a "food pyramid" of content reading that includes traditional textbooks, fiction, trade nonfiction, magazines, and poetry (*apply and extend*).

Other opportunities for teachers to share their work might include maintaining a personal blog or guest blogging for another educator; posting to professional listservs or hashtags; joining social media chats; being a guest on a podcast or creating their own; or writing for a school newsletter, community newspaper, or professional periodical.

As you encounter opportunities for educators to further their work, you can pass these along. If the science chair gets a call for proposals for an upcoming conference, she could simply forward it to her department, but imagine if she included a note to that one teacher, saying something like, "It would be great if you submitted a session on how to create a science classroom library!" Imagine how seen and valued that teacher would feel. Any time you pass along a resource, you have an opportunity to recognize excellent work: "This podcast reminded me of something you said," "I saw this call for manuscripts and thought of your work," or "I thought you might enjoy this article."

Again, you can't do this all the time for everyone, but every little bit counts. Teachers need recognition, not so much in the form of awards or shoutouts or cookies (although no one gets mad at cookies) but in the form of your genuine interest and support so they know their effort, learning, and work matter. *They* matter.

Onward

In this chapter, we saw different ways to assess professional learning, based on different definitions of *effectiveness:* fulfilling objectives, satisfying participants, and promoting a positive faculty culture. We also saw how leaders can contribute to cultural shifts by expressing curiosity about everyone's learning, coaching teachers who struggle or straggle, and furthering teachers who excel. Now that we've explored many ways to assess professional learning and provide differentiated support to teachers, we'll turn in Chapter 6 to the one person on whom we haven't yet focused—you.

The Self-Reflective Curator

As someone who's been to many museums but never worked in one, I used to have a romanticized perception of what curators do. I pictured lots of jet setting, visits to spacious art lofts, intellectual conversations where people used words like *hegemony* and *oeuvre*, and opening nights with craft cocktails. In my naive mind, curation was a movie starring Timothée Chalamet and a bunch of other well-groomed millennials.

Real-life curation isn't so glitzy—not for art and certainly not for PD. In fact, curating PD adds to your workload in at least three ways. First, organizing in-house PD will demand more time and effort than outsourcing your professional learning needs to a speaker or consultant. Second, curating PD might mean dealing with teachers who aren't happy with the topic, the process, or the mere fact of having to do the work. And because in-house PD makes people vulnerable, you might see more people acting out as they try to avoid the struggles associated with it, which means you, as the leader, will need to deal with them. Finally, just like anything else, curating professional learning requires practice. Especially when you first get started, you might find less payoff for all your hard work than you might like. Curation can stress us out before, during, and after the fact.

This maybe isn't such an inspiring way to end a book about curating PD. Shouldn't I be sending you on your way with some motivating words about how this work will energize your school culture and amplify student learning? But acting in accordance with our values usually means accepting some pain and struggle into our lives. Maybe you sometimes hear implicit messages that you're not supposed to feel certain emotions, and if you do, you shouldn't show them because it's unprofessional. As a leader who cares, you naturally open yourself to feelings of doubt, worry, and fear if there's any chance things won't go well—and to feelings of disappointment, anger, and sadness when things don't go as well as you would've liked.

Those feelings are not signs of weakness. They're signs of strength. They mean your values are at stake. That's why this chapter isn't going to give you a pep talk on curating PD. Instead, it will offer ways for you to check in with your values so even when you struggle or fail, you'll remember why this work was important to you in the first place and why it's worth continuing to do—not because your reputation is riding on it or because you want to please one of your many constituencies but because it matters to you and is part of being the leader you want to be.

Recognizing Your Leadership Values

Psychology professor Kelly Wilson defines *values* as "freely chosen, verbally constructed consequences of ongoing, dynamic, evolving patterns of activity, which establish predominant reinforcers for that activity that are intrinsic in engagement in the valued behavioral pattern itself" (Wilson & DuFrene, 2009, p. 64). For our purposes, we can use a simpler version of Wilson's definition: values are *qualities of action that matter to us*.

As qualities of action, values describe *how* we do things—including teaching, running meetings, making disciplinary decisions, and anything else an educational leader does in or beyond school. To name qualities of action, we need adverbs. You can teach *creatively,* run meetings *compassionately,* make disciplinary decisions *inclusively,* and—as a PD curator—plan events *respectfully,* explain protocols *enthusiastically,* and measure effectiveness *persistently.* You can find examples of values, stated as qualities of action, in Figure 6.1 (adapted from Porosoff & Weinstein, 2018, p. 214). Which values feel especially important to you?

At some point, maybe you went to a leadership training and were given a list of values like this one (although they were probably abstract nouns such as *creativity* and *generosity,* as opposed to adverbs such as *creatively* and *generously*), and you were asked to identify a few that resonated with you. Alternatively, maybe you were given the words on cards and sorted them based on their importance to you.

Choosing from lists and sorting cards aren't great ways to clarify values. These adverbs (and their abstract noun cousins) aren't things you can see or visualize. You can't scroll through your photo stream and spot *creatively* or encounter *generously* in

---

FIGURE 6.1

Examples of Values as Qualities of Action

actively	diligently	inclusively	reasonably
adventurously	efficiently	independently	resiliently
ambitiously	enthusiastically	kindly	resourcefully
appreciatively	fairly	knowledgeably	respectfully
assertively	flexibly	lovingly	responsibly
authentically	forgivingly	loyally	reverently
attentively	generously	modestly	seriously
carefully	gracefully	open-mindedly	skillfully
compassionately	gratefully	patiently	spiritually
considerately	helpfully	peacefully	steadily
cooperatively	honestly	perceptively	supportively
courageously	honorably	persistently	thoroughly
creatively	hopefully	playfully	traditionally
curiously	humbly	practically	trustworthily
decisively	humorously	precisely	warmly
deliberately	imaginatively	productively	wisely

Source: From *EMPOWER Your Students* (p. 214), by L. Porosoff and J. Weinstein, 2018. Bloomington, IN: Solution Tree. Copyright 2018 Solution Tree. Reprinted with permission.

the hallways of your school. You can look for people behaving creatively or generously, but those actions can look like a lot of different things. You could probably list 10 different ways a school leader could behave creatively or generously. If you asked a colleague to list 10 different ways to behave creatively or generously at work, that person might come up with an entirely different list. You yourself might come up with an entirely different list next week.

The point is, there are many different actions to which you could apply these qualities, and there are many different ways you could apply the qualities to those actions. A list of adverbs doesn't really help us understand or recognize what values-consistent living looks and feels like. A better way to clarify your leadership values would be to think of some of the times in your work when you felt a sense of meaning and purpose, vividly imagining what you saw and heard and felt, and then try to identify the qualities you brought to your actions in those moments.

Remember: the very actions that bring us meaning and vitality will also bring the full range of our emotions. As Kelly Wilson put it, "Values and vulnerabilities are always poured from the same vessel" (Wilson & DuFrene, 2009, p. 67). Anything meaningful—including the meaningful work of curating professional development at your school—will sometimes be painful, but if you're willing to explore your struggles, you'll find your values.

Bringing Your Leadership Values to PD Curation

The three exercises that follow will help you relate differently to your struggles by connecting them to your values. In To-Do List Appraisal, you give values-based ratings to the various tasks you need to do. The Responding to Disruptive Behavior exercise helps you do just that: act in accordance with your values when a faculty member derails, disrespects, or otherwise hinders professional learning. Finally, in Values Alignment Check, you identify some of your leadership values, consider how you enact those values while curating PD, and notice opportunities to bring your values to future work. None of these exercises will make your struggles magically go away, but they'll all help you dignify those struggles by understanding the values you want to bring to curating professional learning—and to your leadership in general.

To-Do List Appraisal

This book provides possibilities, not mandates. It's not necessary to use every tool and protocol to improve professional learning at your school. It's not even *advisable* to use every idea. Rather, you should use the ones that work for you, your faculty, and your timeframe. This exercise helps you prioritize tasks according to your own values so the time and effort you spend curating PD feels worthwhile.

Exercise

- Look at Figure 6.2. In the first column, make a list of the things you currently need to do to design, implement, assess, or otherwise support professional learning at your school.
- In the *Excitement* column, give each task a rating on a scale of 1 to 10, based on how excited you are to complete it.

- In the *Confidence* column, give each task a rating on a scale of 1 to 10, based on how confident you are that you can complete the task under your current circumstances.
- In the *Importance* column, give each task a rating on a scale of 1 to 10, based on how important it is in bringing about good professional learning (based on your own definition of what makes professional learning *good*).

FIGURE 6.2

To-Do List Ratings

To-Do List	Excitement	Confidence	Importance

Reflection Questions

- For items that have higher *Importance* ratings than *Excitement* ratings: Why will a future version of you be glad you took these actions?
- For items that have higher *Importance* ratings than *Confidence* ratings: What concerns do you have? What kinds of support will you need to accomplish these tasks to your satisfaction? Who can provide that support?
- Even if you don't accomplish these tasks to your satisfaction, why might they still be worth trying?
- Just because something is on your to-do list doesn't always mean you have to do it. Is there anything on your list you can either delegate to someone who'd benefit from the leadership opportunity or simply let go?
- Consider the qualities of action listed in Figure 6.1 (page 110). How can you approach some of the actions on your list in a manner consistent with your values?

Responding to Disruptive Behavior

Good learning experiences push people to confront past assumptions. Any meaningful work can involve tedious, embarrassing, or otherwise unpleasant moments, and peer-to-peer professional learning invokes fears and insecurities that an outsider doesn't. Don't be surprised if in response to all that discomfort, a member of your faculty becomes disruptive.

Some teachers might actively disrupt the PD process, for example by monopolizing a discussion, whispering to others while a colleague delivers a workshop, loudly complaining about how pointless and poorly designed the unit is, or cross-examining you about ideas you're still exploring. But most teachers won't act in these ways—whether out of consideration for others or for fear that they'll look bad (because they will).

More likely, teachers will *passively* disrupt the PD process. They'll "forget" to fill out surveys or attend meetings, decline invitations to share their ideas, claim they have nothing to contribute, actually think they have nothing to contribute, or wear charmingly passive-aggressive facial expressions when certain colleagues speak.

Perhaps you can imagine other ways teachers might actively or passively disrupt the PD you've curated—or perhaps you don't have to imagine. Such behaviors are unhelpful at best—and disrespectful, demoralizing, and divisive at worst—but even though it would be easy to label these behaviors as *bad,* you might respond to them differently if you understand them as coming from a place of vulnerability. People who monopolize conversations might fear that their colleagues won't understand their ideas and take them seriously unless they fully explain themselves. People who loudly complain or quietly roll their eyes might feel frustrated that something deeply important to them isn't being discussed or that the same topics keep getting discussed with no actual change. These feelings don't excuse bad behavior, but they do help us understand where people are coming from.

It's totally understandable to feel annoyed and frustrated, if not outright angry and disgusted, when people behave in these ways. As a leader, you might feel pressured to appear calm and sound positive all the time, and you might get the implicit message—if not the explicit one—that emotions such as anger and disgust should be managed and controlled, or even that there's something wrong with you if you feel them at all.

Remember that emotions are powerful indicators that something important is at stake. If you feel annoyed or angry when teachers refuse to participate productively, it means something you care about is being threatened. In this case, what's being threatened is the learning community—and ultimately the learning itself. Meanwhile, if teachers feel afraid or upset and are acting out in response, it means that something *they* care about is being threatened. Even though you might feel as if you're at odds with these faculty members, you might have some of the same emotions and values. If nothing else, you both *have* emotions and values, and noticing that common experience can help you have a different kind of conversation and build a different kind of relationship.

This exercise won't prevent teachers from disrupting the professional learning experiences you curate. It also won't give you any magic words to make them stop. It will, however, help you reflect on where their behaviors might be coming from and connect with them in a values-consistent way that respects and empowers both of you.

For the exercise, you'll need a copy of the Circles of Compassion worksheet (Figure 6.3), a pen, and a *very* open mind.

Exercise

- Think of a teacher who has done something to disrupt the professional learning process—for themselves, someone else, or the community as a whole. Although you might think of this person's behaviors as a *problem,* chances are that for them, the behaviors are a *solution.* That person is experiencing unwanted feelings, and the behaviors are helping make those feelings go away. What might some of those feelings be? You don't know for sure, even if you ask, but based on what you know about this person and what you've seen so far, what emotions might this person be experiencing? Write these in Quadrant 1.

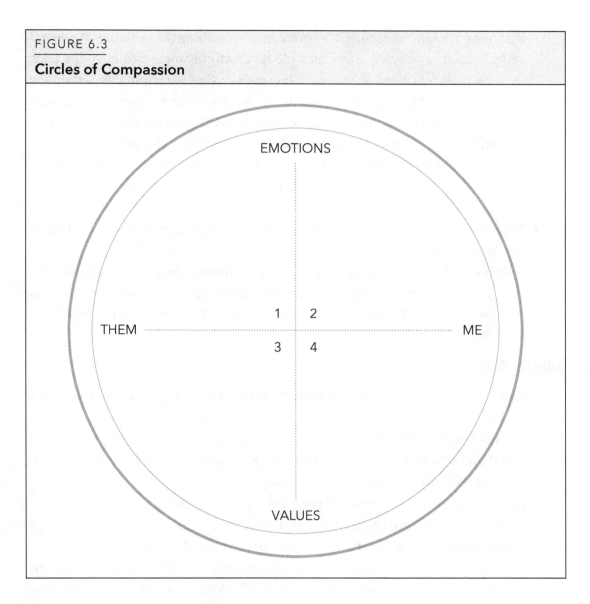

FIGURE 6.3

Circles of Compassion

- If this person is behaving disruptively, then *you* might have certain feelings when you talk to, encounter, or even think about them. Maybe you've gotten the message that you're supposed to remain calm and professional at all times, but that doesn't mean you don't or shouldn't have emotions. What emotions do you experience when you interact with or just think about this person? Write these in Quadrant 2.

- Emotions are information. They reveal that something important is at stake. If we feel afraid or worried, it can mean that something important might be taken from us. If we feel angry or annoyed, it can mean that something important *was* taken from us. If we feel sad, it can mean that something important is gone. If we feel disgusted or bored, it can mean that something important that should be happening isn't. If we feel disappointed, it can mean we expected someone to do something important, and they didn't. Reflect on what the other person's emotions reveal about what important things could be at stake for them. Write these in Quadrant 3.
- Reflect on what your emotions reveal about what important things are at stake for you. Write these in Quadrant 4.
- Reflect on what you and this person have in common—in terms of specific emotions you both have, specific things or conditions you both seem to care about, or even just the fact of having emotions and values. Write these commonalities in the outer circle.

Reflection Questions

- Based on the commonalities you discovered, how can you connect with this person?
- Psychologist Paul Gilbert (2017) defines *compassion* as "a sensitivity to suffering in self and others with a commitment to try to alleviate and prevent it" (p. 11). How are both you and this person suffering?
- What can you do to alleviate and prevent this person's suffering?
- What can you do to alleviate and prevent your own suffering?
- How important is it to you to lead with compassion and self-compassion?
- Regardless of the outcome, what values do you want to enact when having a conversation with this teacher? You may wish to look at the qualities of action listed in Figure 6.1 (page 110) as you answer this question.

Values Alignment Check

For this exercise, you'll identify qualities you think are most important to bring to your actions as a leader. Then you'll think of specific times when you succeeded and struggled to enact these qualities. Finally, you'll write about these times in the Enacting My Leadership Values chart (Figure 6.4).

FIGURE 6.4

Enacting My Leadership Values

Qualities of action that matter to you in your leadership	As you designed and implemented this professional learning, what was something you did especially ___?	As you designed and implemented this professional learning, what was something you struggled or failed to do ___?
1.		
2.		
3.		
4.		

As you write about your experiences, you might find yourself reveling in the joy of success and pushing away the pain of failure—or wallowing in it, as the case may be. You might also find yourself defending your actions or seeking someone's affirmation that what you did was actually OK. These kinds of behaviors are understandable, but they can get in the way of values-consistent action (Hayes, Strosahl, & Wilson, 2012). Instead of clinging to pleasant thoughts and pushing away unpleasant ones, try to notice any emotions you feel.

Exercise

- Look at the qualities of action listed in Figure 6.1 (page 110). Choose four of these qualities that feel especially important for you to bring to your actions as a leader, and write them in the first column of the Enacting My Leadership Values chart. If there's a quality that matters to you but isn't on the list, feel free to write it in your chart. The list of values is here to help you, not limit you.
- Think back on the things you've done so far to design and implement professional learning for your faculty. What was something you did especially _____? (Fill in the blank with each value you wrote in the first column, and write responses to the four resulting questions.)
- Continue to reflect on what you've done to design and implement professional learning for your faculty. What was something you struggled or failed to do _____? (Fill in the blank with each value you wrote in the first column, and write responses to the four resulting questions.)

Reflection Questions

- When you successfully enacted your values, how did you feel? How do you feel looking back on those moments now? What was the impact on others?
- When you struggled to enact each value, what got in the way?
- What can you learn about curating PD from your successes? From your struggles?
- What can you learn about yourself from your successes? From your struggles?
- As you continue to curate professional learning experiences for your faculty, what can you do to enact these values more fully?
- How do you bring these values to other aspects of your leadership, beyond PD curation?

Building a Team of Curators

For sure, curating PD adds to your workload, but that doesn't mean you have to do it all or that you have to do it alone. Building a great professional learning team not only allows you to share these burdens but might even make the work fun. More than that, the members of a professional learning curation team can benefit from one another's expertise and learn how to curate together. Curating professional learning can *be* professional learning.

Conclusion:
Stepping into the Curator Role

The word *curate* is a back-formation of the word *curator*. That is, first came the curator—the person who took care of the art, understood its history, selected pieces with care, and organized the exhibit—and only later did we get the word *curate* to describe these actions with a single verb. Before the act of curating came the role of curator.

You already have a role. Maybe you're the principal, the chair of the English department, or the dean of 9th grade students. Maybe you occupy multiple roles—you're the assistant superintendent for curriculum and instruction *and* the assessment data coordinator. Your current role already gives you enough to do. Yet there's a difference between a person's role and their work. What's the work you're doing at your school–the larger purpose you're trying to serve—which perhaps led you to take on your current role in the first place? How can the curator role help you further that work?.

There's one last lesson about curation we can learn from those for whom it's an official job and not just something done with YouTube videos and wedding guests. Curators don't just select and arrange other people's art; they *are* artists. They create something—an exhibition, an event, a professional learning experience—that is itself beautiful, powerful, and important.

In education, we easily get caught up in crises or in the drudgery of meetings, spreadsheets, and phone calls. If that's true of teachers, it might be even more true of administrators who don't get the pleasure of watching a child's face almost literally light up with the joy of discovery or of reading a parent's thank-you note at the end of a tough year.

Curating allows you to bring creativity to your work. Beyond the ways engaging in peer-to-peer PD elevates the work of participating teachers, curating it elevates the work of the person who designs it. It makes you—in addition to being a boss, a manager, or even a leader—an artist.

References

Alpers, S. (1991). The museum as a way of seeing. In I. Karp & S. D. Lavine (Eds.), *Exhibiting cultures: The poetics and politics of museum display* (pp. 25–32). Washington, DC: Smithsonian Institution.

Asch, D. A., & Rosin, R. (2016). Engineering social incentives for health. *New England Journal of Medicine, 375*(26), 2511–2513.

Barnes-Holmes, D., Hayes, S. C., & Dymond, S. (2001). Self and self-directed rules. In S. C. Hayes, D. Barnes-Holmes, & B. Roche (Eds.), *Relational frame theory: A post-Skinnerian account of human language and cognition* (pp. 119–139). New York: Kluwer Academic/Plenum.

Bedford, L. (2016). *The art of museum exhibitions: How story and imagination create aesthetic experiences*. New York: Routledge.

Bell, L. A. (2008). Expanding definitions of "good teaching." In M. Pollock (Ed.). *Everyday antiracism: Getting real about race in school.* (pp. 287–290). New York: New Press.

Bergmann, J., & Sams, A. (2012). *Flip your classroom: Reach every student in every class every day*. Eugene, OR: International Society for Technology in Education.

Brown, B. A. (2019). *Science in the city: Culturally relevant STEM education*. Cambridge, MA: Harvard Education Press.

Della Flora, O. (2019). Creative ways to get kids to thrive in school [video file]. Retrieved from https://www .ted.com/talks/olympia_della_flora_creative_ways_to_get_kids_to_thrive_in_school

Dennis-Yarmouth Regional School District (n.d.). Our core values and beliefs. Retrieved from www.dy-regional .k12.ma.us/district/office-superintendent/pages/our-core-values-and-beliefs

Edcamp Foundation. (n.d.). Join the Movement. Edcamp Community. Retrieved from www.edcamp.org/attend

Ellington Public Schools (2016). Core values and beliefs. Retrieved from www.ellingtonpublicschools.org/ schools/ellington-high-school/academics/core-values-and-beliefs

Elson, K. (2019). How should we sing happy birthday? *Rethinking Schools, 33*(3), 52–57.

Falk, J. H. (2016). *Identity and the museum visitor experience*. New York: Taylor & Francis.

Falk, J. H., & Dierking, L. D. (2018). *Learning from museums* (2nd ed.). Lanham, MD: Rowman & Littlefield.

Foody, M., Barnes-Holmes, Y., & Barnes-Holmes, D. (2012). The role of self in acceptance & commitment therapy. In L. McHugh & I. Stewart (Eds.), *The self and perspective taking: Contributions and applications from modern behavioral science* (pp. 125–142). Oakland, CA: New Harbinger.

Gilbert, P. (2017). Compassion: Definitions and controversies. In P. Gilbert (Ed.), *Compassion: Concepts, research, and applications* (pp. 3–15). London: Routledge.

Golding, W. (2016). *Lord of the flies*. New York: Penguin. (Original work published 1959)

Goodlander, M. R. (1921). *Education through experience: A four-year experiment in the ethical culture school.* New York: Bureau of Educational Experiments.

Hayes, S. C., Barlow, D. H., & Nelson-Gray, R. O. (1999). *The scientist practitioner: Research and accountability in the age of managed care.* New York: Allyn & Bacon.

Hayes, S. C., Gifford, E. V., Townsend, R. C., & Barnes-Holmes, D. (2001). Thinking, problem-solving, and pragmatic verbal analysis. In S. C. Hayes, D. Barnes-Holmes, & B. Roche (Eds.), *Relational frame theory: A post-Skinnerian account of human language and cognition* (pp. 87-102). New York: Kluwer Academic/ Plenum.

Hayes, S. C., Strosahl, K., & Wilson, K. G. (1999). *Acceptance and commitment therapy: An experiential approach to behavior change.* New York: Guilford

Hayes, S. C., Strosahl, K., & Wilson, K. G. (2012). *Acceptance and commitment therapy: The process and practice of mindful change* (2nd ed.). New York: Guilford.

Jennings, P. A. (2018). *The trauma-sensitive classroom: Building resilience with compassionate teaching.* New York: W. W. Norton & Company.

Krathwohl, D. R. (2002). A revision of Bloom's taxonomy: An overview. *Theory into Practice, 41*(4), 212-218.

Love, B. L. (2019). *We want to do more than survive: Abolitionist teaching and the pursuit of educational freedom.* Boston: Beacon.

Lubar, S. D. (2017). *Inside the lost museum: Curating, past and present.* Cambridge, MA: Harvard University Press.

Luciano, C., Valdiva-Salas, S., & Ruiz, F. (2012). The self as the context for rule-governed behavior. In L. McHugh & I. Stewart (Eds.), *The self and perspective taking: Contributions and applications from modern behavioral science* (pp. 143-160). Oakland, CA: New Harbinger.

Mankato Area Public Schools (n.d.). Core values. Retrieved from www.isd77.org/discover-maps/about-maps /core-values

McDonald, J. P., Mohr, N., Dichter, A., & McDonald, E. C. (2015). *The power of protocols: An educator's guide to better practice* (3rd ed.). New York: Teachers College Press.

McHugh, L., Stewart, I., & Almada, P. (2019). *A contextual behavioral guide to the self: Theory and practice.* Oakland, CA: Context Press.

Miller, W. R., & Rollnick, S. (2013). *Motivational interviewing: Helping people change* (3rd ed.). New York: Guilford.

Milner, H. R., Cunningham, H. B., Delale-O'Connor, L., & Kestenberg, E. G. (2018). *"These kids are out of control": Why we must reimagine "classroom management" for equity.* Thousand Oaks, CA: Corwin.

Muir, J. (2004). *My first summer in the Sierra.* Mineola, NY: Dover.

Nellen, T. (n.d.). I heard, I noticed, I wondered [blog post]. Retrieved from www.tnellen.com/cybereng/method .html

Nieto, S. & Bode, P. (2017). *Affirming diversity: The sociopolitical context of multicultural education* (7th ed.). Boston: Pearson/Allyn & Bacon.

Porosoff, L. (2014). Systems vs. heaps: Aligning professional development to school values. *Independent School, 74*(1), 110-114.

Porosoff, L. (2017). The power of in-house professional development. *Independent School, 76*(1), 30-36.

Porosoff, L. (2020). *Teach meaningful: Tools to design the curriculum at your core.* Lanham, MD: Rowman & Littlefield.

Porosoff, L., & Weinstein, J. (2018). *EMPOWER your students: Tools to inspire a meaningful learning experience.* Bloomington, IN: Solution Tree.

Porosoff, L., & Weinstein, J. (2020). *Two-for-one teaching: Connecting instruction to student values.* Bloomington, IN: Solution Tree.

Reilly, M. (2018). *Curatorial activism: Towards an ethics of curating.* New York: Thames & Hudson.

Rubin, A., & Salmieri, D. (2012). *Dragons love tacos.* New York: Penguin Young Readers Group.

Schwarz, N., & Oyserman, D. (2001). Asking questions about behavior: Cognition, communication, and questionnaire construction. *American Journal of Evaluation, 22*(2), 127-160.

Simon, N. (2010). *The participatory museum*. Santa Cruz, CA: Museum 2.0.

Smith, D., Fisher, D., & Frey, N. (2015). *Better than carrots or sticks: Restorative practices for positive classroom management*. Alexandria, VA: ASCD.

Thompson Falls Public Schools (2013). Core values. Retrieved from www.thompsonfalls.net/Page/785

Waltz, T. J., & Follette, W. C. (2009). Molar functional relations and clinical behavior analysis: Implications for assessment and treatment. *The Behavior Analyst, 32*(1), 51–68.

Wiggins, G., & McTighe, J. (2005). *Understanding by design* (2nd ed.). Alexandria, VA: ASCD.

Wilson, K. G., & DuFrene, T. (2009). *Mindfulness for two: An acceptance and commitment therapy approach to mindfulness in psychotherapy*. Oakland, CA: New Harbinger.

Index

The letter *f* following a page number denotes a figure.

About the Author

Lauren Porosoff presents and consults on how to create inclusive and empowering learning communities. An educator with 18 years of classroom experience, Lauren has developed applications of contextual behavioral science to various education practices, including instructional design, social-emotional learning, and professional development. She is the lead author of *EMPOWER Your Students: Tools to Inspire a Meaningful School Experience* (Solution Tree, 2018), *Two-for-One Teaching: Connecting Instruction to Student Values* (Solution Tree, 2020), and *Teach Meaningful: Tools to Design the Curriculum at Your Core* (Rowman & Littlefield, 2020).

Lauren has written for *AMLE Magazine, Independent School, Phi Delta Kappan, Rethinking Schools,* and *Teaching Tolerance* about how students and teachers can bring their values to their learning, work, and relationships at school. She has presented on these topics at conferences of various professional organizations, including ASCD, Learning & the Brain, NCTE, and NAESP. She regularly offers longer workshops for regional associations of independent schools, including ISACS, NJAIS, NCAIS, NWAIS, NYSAIS, and VAIS. She received a bachelor's degree in English from Wesleyan University and a law degree from George Washington University. She lives in New York with her co-everything, Jonathan Weinstein, her two spectacular children, her extremely generous parents, and a cat named Benedict.

Learn more about Lauren's work at empowerforwards.com, and follow her on Twitter at @LaurenPorosoff.

Related ASCD Resources: Professional Development

At the time of publication, the following resources were available (ASCD stock numbers in parentheses).

Adventures in Teacher Leadership: Pathways, Strategies, and Inspiration for Every Teacher by Rebecca Mieliwocki and Joseph Fatheree (#118033)

The Burnout Cure: Learning to Love Teaching Again by Chase Mielke (#119004)

Coherent School Leadership: Forging Clarity from Complexity by Michael Fullan and Lyle Kirtman (#118040)

C.R.A.F.T. Conversations for Teacher Growth: How to Build Bridges and Cultivate Expertise by Sally J. Zepeda, Lakesha Robinson Goff, and Stefanie W. Steele (#120001)

Creating a Culture of Reflective Practice: Capacity-Building for Schoolwide Success by Pete Hall and Alisa Simeral (#117006)

Facilitating Teacher Teams and Authentic PLCs: The Human Side of Leading People, Protocols, and Practices by Daniel R. Venables (#117004)

Insights into Action: Successful School Leaders Share What Works by William Sterrett (#112009)

Leadership for Learning: How to Bring Out the Best in Every Teacher, 2nd Edition by Carl Glickman and Rebecca West Burns (#121007)

Leading Change Together: Developing Educator Capacity Within Schools and Systems by Eleanor Drago-Severson and Jessica Blum-DeStefano (#117027)

The Learning Leader: How to Focus School Improvement for Better Results, 2nd Edition by Douglas B. Reeves (#118003)

Personalized Professional Learning: A Job-Embedded Pathway for Elevating Teacher Voice by Allison Rodman (#118028)

Teacher-Centered Professional Development by Gabriel Diaz-Maggioli (#104021)

For up-to-date information about ASCD resources, go to www.ascd.org. You can search the complete archives of *Educational Leadership* at www.ascd.org/el.

ASCD myTeachSource®
Download resources from a professional learning platform with hundreds of research-based best practices and tools for your classroom at http://myteachsource.ascd.org/

For more information, send an e-mail to member@ascd.org; call 1-800-933-2723 or 703-578-9600; send a fax to 703-575-5400; or write to Information Services, ASCD, 1703 N. Beauregard St., Alexandria, VA 22311-1714 USA.

WHOLE CHILD
TENETS

1 HEALTHY
Each student enters school
healthy and learns about and
practices a healthy lifestyle.

2 SAFE
Each student learns in an
environment that is physically
and emotionally safe for
students and adults.

3 ENGAGED
Each student is actively
engaged in learning and is
connected to the school and
broader community.

4 SUPPORTED
Each student has access to
personalized learning and is
supported by qualified,
caring adults.

5 CHALLENGED
Each student is challenged
academically and prepared
for success in college or
further study and for
employment and participation
in a global environment.

THE WHOLE CHILD

The ASCD Whole Child approach is an effort to transition
from a focus on narrowly defined academic achievement to
one that promotes the long-term development and success
of all children. Through this approach, ASCD supports
educators, families, community members, and policymakers
as they move from a vision about educating the whole child
to sustainable, collaborative actions.

The PD Curator relates to the **engaged**, **supported** and
challenged tenets.

*For more about the ASCD Whole Child approach, visit **www.
ascd.org/wholechild.***

Become an ASCD member today!
Go to www.ascd.org/joinascd
or call toll-free: 800-933-ASCD (2723)

LEARN. TEACH. LEAD.

CPSIA information can be obtained
at www.ICGtesting.com
Printed in the USA
LVHW062008230323
742386LV00020B/172